ROLLS ROYCE & BENTLEY

Graham Robson

© Colin Gower Enterprises Ltd

Published by

kp books
An Imprint of F+W Publications

700 East State Street • Iola, WI 54990-0001
715-445-2214 • 888-457-2873

Library of Congress Catalog Number: 2005906861

ISBN: 0-89689-238-7

Edited by Ed Myers

Designed by Mark Roberts, Talking Design Ltd

Printed in China

CONTENTS

INTRODUCTION

This is a very complicated story. In more than 100 years, not only were Rolls-Royce and Bentley first independent, then together, and finally separated again; over the years the cars have been assembled in no fewer than six different factories. In the early years, the companies could maintain themselves, but from 1980 were happy to cuddle up to Vickers Ltd., the giant shipbuilding, engineering, and armaments conglomerate. Then came 1998, the major sale, and the split of Rolls-Royce from Bentley, in which they separately became subsidiaries of massive German parent companies.

But there is more. Until the 1930s, the car brands were dominant, but aircraft engine manufacture then became more important, and from 1973 the cars business was separated completely from that of aircraft engine building. Confused? Many automotive, aeronautical, or business experts have often found this process difficult to understand.

Growing up

Rolls-Royce and Bentley were totally separate companies until 1931:

In the beginning the Rolls-Royce marque was set up in 1904, when Henry Royce, lacking cash and backing to build the cars he knew he could design, met up with the Hon. Charles Rolls, an aristocrat and motoring enthusiast who was already an experienced motor trader. Originally from Royce's factory at Cooke Street in Manchester, in northern England, then, from 1908, from a brand new factory in Derby, some 50 miles to the southeast, the new cars made a fine reputation for themselves. The massive 40/50hp, soon known as the "Silver Ghost" (even though some purists state that there was only ever one Silver Ghost – that owned by the factory), set so many new standards that it would soon be known as the "Best Car in the World."

Once established at Derby, Rolls-Royce made sure that its chassis were designed, developed, and constructed as well, and as carefully as possible. (Body design and construction was left to specialists outside the firm until the late 1940s). If there were two ways of doing anything, the best way, not the cost-cutting way, would always be chosen, which may explain why a Rolls-Royce has always been one of the world's most expensive cars.

Following their meeting in 1904, the Hon.. Charles Stewart Rolls (right) and Frederick Henry Royce set up the Rolls-Royce marque, which has now been in business for over 100 years.

Rolls-Royce chassis assembly at the Derby factory in the 1920s, with both Twenty (horizontal radiator slats) and 40/50hp Silver Ghost (mesh) radiator grilles in view. Rolls-Royce did not build its own body shells at this time.

Throughout the 1920s, steady and mostly prudent expansion gave the company a peerless brand image. That image was of providing the best possible cars for their job – not the fastest, and not the most visually attractive, but simply the best-built machines that Rolls-Royce could devise.

Although there was one important miscalculation – the failure to establish a permanent manufacturing presence in the United States – this would soon be forgotten when the chance came to buy the remains of the troubled Bentley concern.

Intent on producing fine sports cars to match any other automobile in the world, W.O. Bentley founded his new Bentley company in 1919, and began deliveries of 3-Liter models in 1921. Like Rolls-Royce at this time, the company never produced bodies. Although Bentley's Cricklewood factory was new, and its staff first-rate, the business was always underfinanced, and profits were difficult to find. Not even a burgeoning and successful motor racing program could boost sales far enough to change the bottom line consistently to black.

Before the end of the 1920s, Bentley had built up a fine mechanical reputation on the back of cars like the 6$^{1}/_{2}$-liter Speed Six, and the 4$^{1}/_{2}$-liter, but at the same time the company's finances had needed frequent

Right from the start, W.O. Bentley (center) used motor sport to advertise his cars. A 3-liter won the Le Mans 24-Hour race of 1924, driven by Frank Clement (left) and Capt. John Duff.

injections of capital. About this time, playboy/race driver Woolf Barnato became chairman at Bentley. W.O. Bentley always insisted that the racing program was financially justified – and four straight wins at Le Mans from 1927 to 1930 may prove his point – but the Depression hit Bentley hard, and as sales fell, it was forced into receivership in 1931.

Before the end of the year, the remains of the company had been put up for sale. After a sordid courtroom battle a shadowy organization called the "British Central Equitable Trust," made the highest bid – and almost immediately delivered Bentley into the hands of Rolls-Royce.

Together for seventy years

And so it was that Bentley and Rolls-Royce came

together, the two brands being progressively integrated. They would remain in each other's arms until 1998.

Rolls-Royce gradually modernized its chassis and encouraged change to the styling of the coachwork. Other than that, there were no hasty innovations. Bentley, on the other hand, was transformed. All traces of W.O./Cricklewood-type engineering was swept aside, the factory was sold off, and from 1933 there was a new type of Bentley, based on Rolls-Royce engineering, and dubbed "The Silent Sports Car."

Thus revitalized, the twin marques carried on steadily until 1939, when Adolf Hitler's armies marched into Poland and changed the world forever. Rolls-Royce then concentrated on building massive and magnificent aircraft engines to power warplanes, and made them at a new factory in Crewe, in northwestern England.

From this point, the aircraft engine business (piston or gas-turbine) was always larger, more important, and more profitable than that of building cars. Indeed, at one time the directors thought of abandoning car manufacture completely, especially as it was also developing nonautomotive diesel engines and a range of military vehicle engines.

It was not until 1946, when peace had returned to the world, that Crewe became the center of car-building

By 1998, Rolls-Royce had remodeled the front entrance of its fifty year-old main administration block. This artist's impression showed the new entrance, in front of a foyer that always included at least one new car on display.

operations, which it has been to this day. A new product strategy saw all postwar cars engineered around a single new chassis, made in several wheelbase lengths, and for the first time with cars clad in a standard steel body shell (first on Bentley, later on Rolls-Royce).

In two postwar decades, the company produced only two different chassis and basic body styles, but special coachwork, sporting Bentleys, and massive coach-built limousines all added variety to the product line.. Although an all-new alloy V-8 engine was introduced in 1959, technical progress was otherwise measured and deliberate (slow, some said), for Rolls-Royce always preferred to refine and perfect the known, rather than to gamble on the trendy and unproven. As

Technical Director Harry Grylls once said in the 1960s, when asked why Rolls-Royce did not adopt disc brakes:

"We will fit them when they are good enough, quiet enough, and as reliable as our existing brakes . . ."

Until the 1960s, more Bentleys were sold than Rolls-Royces, but that balance then shifted inexorably. After the new-type monocoque Silver Shadow generation of cars appeared in 1965, Rolls-Royce was in the ascendant, and by 1980 Bentley again in the shadows. In the meantime, the Rolls-Royce Company had gone through a cataclysmic industrial trauma, when an important new aircraft engine project (the RB211) had hit technical problems, and dragged the business down into receivership in 1971.

With vital military projects at risk, the British government had to intervene to keep the company alive, and as a result, the automobile business was floated off into independence in 1973. The aircraft engine business recovered rapidly, and was eventually returned to private ownership. By the end of the century, it had become one of the world's largest and most prestigious makers of gas-turbine power units.

At the same time, the aircraft-engine business always retained the overall trademark rights to the Rolls-Royce brand, an asset that was to become vitally important in 1998 and thereafter.

In 1973, funds were found – somehow – to engineer a new range of cars, the Silver Spirit/Mulsanne generation. Seven years of independence followed. Even so, in 1980, when Vickers Ltd., the prestigious British engineering-manufacturing group, made friendly approaches about a takeover, these overtures were speedily accepted.

Vickers' ownership was benign, though they always kept tight control on investment spending. As a result, most new models produced in the 1980s and 1990s were developments of the original Silver Spirit range, rather than anything radically new. In marketing terms, though, the big news was the adoption of turbocharged engines, and the major revival of the Bentley brand. At the same time, Vickers took control of Cosworth, the noted race and high-performance road car engine builder based in Northampton, in central England. There was little attempt, however, to merge Cosworth with Rolls-Royce at Crewe.

By the 1990s, though, Vickers had concluded that Rolls-Royce/Bentley could not prosper on its own forever. For a new generation of cars, Vickers had already decided to buy new engines from another manufacturer. (After a proposed affair with Mercedes-Benz went sour, the engine supply contract went to BMW of Germany.) The twin models – Rolls-Royce Silver Seraph and Bentley Arnage – would be ready for launch in 1998, but after that Vickers would be ready to let go.

In fact, even before the new cars were ready for sale, Vickers knew that the business at Crewe had to be sold off to a larger company – an automotive company, even – that could protect the brands in the new century. With several prestigious German companies – BMW, Mercedes-Benz, and VW – all interested in taking control, the corporate shake-out that followed fascinated financial pundits everywhere. I cover this in more detail in "Running Battle," after Chapter 6.

After 67 years of unity, though, the end result was that Bentley was captured by VW and Rolls-Royce by BMW. Bentley remained at Crewe, while Rolls-Royce eventually moved to a new factory at Goodwood in Sussex, in southeastern England. Both brands were revised, both were refashioned to reflect their new owners' ambitions, and both entered the new century with high hopes. This survey, therefore, comes just in time, for within ten more years I have no doubt that all evidence of previous cooperation will have vanished for ever.

GRAHAM ROBSON 2005

1900s   1910s

TIMELINE

1904: The Rolls-Royce marque founded after The Hon. C.S. Rolls and Henry Royce agreed to combine efforts in making a new car in Manchester in northern England.

1906: Launch of the 40/50hp "Silver Ghost," which established the worldwide reputation of Rolls-Royce.

1908: The business moved from Manchester 50 miles southeast to Derby.

1915: Completion of the first Rolls-Royce "Eagle" aircraft engine. From this time, Rolls-Royce aircraft-engine work would always match automobile evolution.

1919: Engineer Walter Owen Bentley set up Bentley Motors Ltd. at Cricklewood, on the northern outskirts of London. The first Bentley car would be delivered in 1921.

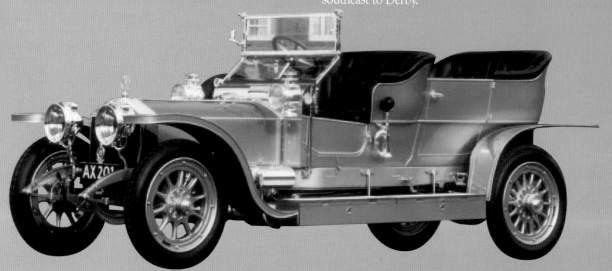

1920s   1930s   1940s

1931: Financial collapse of Bentley. Following a
short period of receivership, Bentley came under the
control of Rolls-Royce Ltd..

1943: Manufacture of Rolls-Royce Derwent gas
turbine ("jet") engines began for use in Gloster Meteor
fighters. Henceforth, aircraft engine building was a
much larger part of the business than producing cars.

1933: Launch of the original
"Rolls-Bentley,"
the 3½-liter model.

1937: Rolls-
Royce Merlin
aircraft engines
went into series
production.

1946: Launch of the Bentley Mk VI, the first-ever
Bentley/Rolls-Royce to have standard steel bodywork.

1939: Rolls-Royce
opened a new factory at
Crewe, to build aircraft
engines. In 1946, this
would become the home
of Rolls-Royce and
Bentley automobiles.

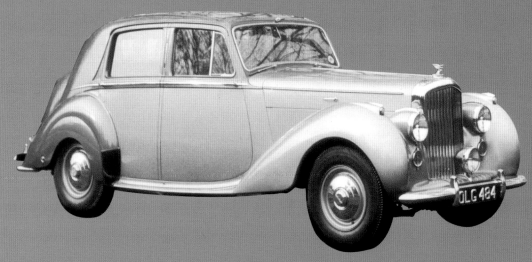

1950s   1960s   1970s

1952: Automatic transmission became available on the cars.

1971: Aircraft engine development problems caused the financial collapse of the parent company. As a result, Rolls-Royce Motor Cars Ltd. was "floated off" into an independent existence in 1973. The Rolls-Royce brand name continued, in parallel, on the revived aircraft engine business.

1959: Introduction of the new V-8 engine, which would be used in almost all Bentleys and Rolls-Royce cars produced for the next forty years.

1965: Introduction of the Silver Shadow/T-Series twins – the company's first-ever car to use a unit-construction monocoque, all-independent suspension, and disc brakes.

SK 90

1980s   1990s   2000s

1980: Rolls-Royce Motor Cars became a subsidiary of Britain's Vickers Group, a large engineering conglomerate.

1982: Introduction of the Bentley Mulsanne Turbo – the first turbocharged car to be put on sale by the company.

2002: VW introduced the VW/Audi-based Bentley four-wheel drive Continental GT coupe; a longer, four-door Continental Flying Spur would follow in 2005. The last Crewe-built Rolls-Royce, and the last to be related to a similar Bentley, was produced.

2003: BMW opened a brand-new Rolls-Royce factory at Goodwood, in Sussex, in southeastern England, and introduced a BMW-based Rolls-Royce called the Phantom.

1998: Vickers sold off the Rolls-Royce and Bentley car-making businesses. After an acrimonious, sometimes farcical, battle, Bentley was acquired by VW of Germany, who retained the Crewe factory, but agreed that the rights to Rolls-Royce would move to BMW, also of Germany, in 2003.

CHAPTER *One*

ROLLS AND ROYCE

SETTING A NEW STANDARD

WHEN FREDERICK HENRY ROYCE WAS BORN IN LINCOLNSHIRE, ENGLAND IN 1863, the first practical motorcars had not even been invented. In 1884, when he and A.E. Clermont set up shop in Manchester, England to build an electrical machinery business, Daimler and Benz of Germany were still not ready to show off their first "horseless carriages." Yet by 1904, when the first three Royce (not Rolls-Royce) cars were constructed, the automobile industry was already a worldwide phenomenon.

Henry Royce knew nothing about engineering until he grew up. First as a flourmill owner's son, then as an apprentice with the Great Northern Railway company, and later as a tester with the Electric Light and Power company of London, he learned for himself. It was only when his final employer went into liquidation in 1884 that he and Claremont set up their own business, at Cooke Street, in Manchester, England.

In the next two decades, Royce and Clermont, as F.H. Royce & Company, clawed their way from rags to riches, first by making dynamos, then by building electric-powered cranes. Along the way, Royce bought

Previous page: The original Royce motor car (the immediate predecessor of the Rolls-Royce) was this two cylinder 10-horsepower of 1904. Only three such cars were built, and none survive.

Above: Rolls-Royce has always been justifiably proud of the company-owned Silver Ghost. (Purists insist that it is the only Silver Ghost, all other types being more accurately called 40/50s.) Here it is following a French-registered example of the late-1950s Silver Cloud.

The 40/50hp Silver Ghost was introduced in 1906, and established the marque as the "Best Car in the World" for the next two decades. This very special derivative of 1907, retained by Rolls-Royce from the day it was produced, was the thirteenth such car built, originally having an aluminum-painted body shell, and silver-plated lamps and fittings.

himself a second-hand (French) Decauville automobile. He spent much time tinkering with it, to make it better and more reliable, and it is often said that the shortcomings of the Decauville led him to design his very first car, the 10-horsepower twin-cylinder Royce. Just three of those cars were produced.

At this point, the Hon. Charles Stewart Rolls enters our story. Rolls, the third son of Lord Llangattock, was already a well-known sportsman and motorist before he opened a garage business, and by 1904 he was operating quite profitably at Brook Street in Mayfair, in the fashionable West End of London. After Henry Edmunds,

Many early-type 40/50hp Silver Ghost models were fitted with impressive limousine coachwork like this.
A long, low hood (left)? Not so – only a very lofty roof line makes it look like that. Details like the lift-out roof
panel and the pleated upholstery were typical of the period.

an intermediary and director of Royce, had told Rolls of the original Royce machines, Rolls met Royce.

After a historic meeting at the Grand Central Hotel, in Manchester, England, Rolls tried a car, liked what he saw, and agreed to take all the cars that Royce could deliver – and that they would be called "Rolls-Royce." Even so, purists who admired the engineer more than the dashing entrepreneur would continue to call the cars "Royces," and it was only in the name-compressing

On a Silver Ghost, the six-cylinder engine was lengthy, and featured side-valve breathing arrangements, Dunlop made clear its patent rights regarding tyres and wheels, and the essential instruments were located well down around the chauffeur's knees.

Rolls-Royce's "Spirit of Ecstasy" radiator mascot is probably the most famous in the automotive world. There have been several different types. Until 1933, all "RR" radiator badges had red lettering.

future that the general public would come to christen such a car a "Rolls" (or, even worse, a "Roller").

Thus, the marque was founded, though a company called Rolls-Royce Limited was not actually established until 1906. Much of the administration, the order, and the method in the new company was applied by Claude Johnson, who was already Rolls's partner in the automobile trade. Johnson would remain, as one of the company's key figures until 1926, when he died of overwork; he was only 61. It was at this time, and with early cars like these, that one of Royce's aphorisms was coined: "The quality remains after the price is forgotten."

In the next few years, Rolls-Royce gradually established itself, not only by making several different cars – 10, 15 and 20-horsepower (with two, three, and four cylinders respectively), a six-cylinder 30-horsepower model, and even V-8-engined oddities called the "Legalimit" and "Invisible Engine" type – but by successfully entering cars in long-distance motor races. Right away, too, the company decided that it knew nothing about producing bodywork, and would have nothing to do with making shells. It was, and would only be, in the business of making rolling chassis for the next forty years. All those chassis were fronted

by that magnificent, and unique, Grecian radiator style — this and the badge containing interwoven "RR" initials made the cars unmistakable.

All this, though, was merely a prelude to further greatness, for in 1906 Royce gathered everything he had so far learned about automotive engineering and designed an all-new car. Riding on a conventional but beautifully detailed chassis, it was initially available in a choice of 135.5 or 143.5 inches long, power was by massive 7.0-liter side-valve six-cylinder engine, which was mated to a four-speed overdrive gearbox. This was the first 40/50hp model, which would soon take up its more familiar name of "Silver Ghost." The car would be Rolls-Royce's flagship model for the next two decades.

Not only was every "Silver Ghost" carefully and painstakingly made, but it was also more reliable and better-looking than almost all of its rivals. Even though the original engine produced no more than 48 horsepower, and the top speed was a mere 50 miles per hour, the clientele did not seem to mind, for the car was uncannily silent and refined, and the approved body styles were almost all elegant. Production never went ahead at an unseemly rate, for individual cars were always built to order, and a customer was often obliged to wait a year or more to take delivery. More than 6,000

would be produced in this way.

It was the thirteenth 40/50hp chassis, tastefully tricked out with an aluminum painted chassis, aluminum paint on the body and with silver plated lamps and fittings, that made its own headlines. Retained by Rolls-Royce as soon as it had been completed, it was the company's proudest possession and mascot for the next ninety years.

Its first use in 1907, though, was to complete a series of magnificent stunts. The first of which was to make a 2,000-mile reliability run, while being observed by the Royal Automobile Club. But it was dwarfed by the second, a 15,000-mile continuous run between London and Glasgow, on differing routes through major towns and cities, non-stop, night-and-day.

This, it was thought, would equate to three years' normal use, but might take only a matter of weeks. After triumphantly completing the reliability run, the Silver Ghost was stripped completely and found to require replacement of only a few minor parts, whose total value was just a few dollars.

Though a late 1920s/early 1930s Rolls-Royce (this was a 20/25-horsepower of the period) was not technologically advanced, it was always beautifully constructed. Details clear in this spread include the comprehensive fascia/instrument display, the immaculate finish of the engine and the engine bay, and the noble detailing of that world-famous grille.

This, and other speed trials and time trials (Rolls, the sportsman, always made sure that his company's claims were backed up by recognized authorities) underpinned the reputation of these costly, but supremely well-built, cars. It wasn't long before the directors were confident enough to adopt the Silver Ghost in a "one model" policy. All earlier Rolls-Royces (which had been thoroughly eclipsed by the 40/50hp car) were dropped, and it was not until 1922 that another new model, the 20-horsepower (sometimes known, tongue-in-cheek, as the "small Rolls-Royce") appeared.

Needing a new factory to produce the Silver Ghost series, Rolls-Royce looked around, and eventually settled on a site in Derby, a town close to the center of England. Opened with a flourish in July 1908 (when Lord Montagu of Beaulieu switched on the electric current to set the machinery in motion), Derby would then be the centre of an ever-growing business until 1939. After that time, it would concentrate on aircraft engine manufacture, which it does to this day.

But it was not all sweetness, light, and success, for grim tidings were to follow. Because the dashing Charles

Rolls had become absorbed in the new-fangled activity of flying in aircraft, he spent less time on Rolls-Royce, and resigned his directorship in April 1910. Only three months later, on July 11, he was flying a Wright biplane in a competition in Bournemouth, crashed it from little more than twenty feet, and was killed instantly.

This, on its own, was a shattering blow, but within a year, there was more to follow. Royce himself, a martyr to overwork and long hours, and to ignoring food and sustenance unless it was put before him, suffered a collapse in health, and had to be dragged permanently away from his beloved workshops and machinery.

That was bad enough, but Royce then suffered what was delicately described as an "intestinal disorder." Even a century later, the whole truth has never emerged, but a malignant tumor was supposed. In consequence, Royce's plumbing had to be rearranged, and for the rest of his life he needed the attention of a full-time nurse, Miss Ethel Aubin.

Even so, Royce made a bargain with Claude Johnson and his colleagues. If they would find him congenial places to live and work, at a reduced pace, he would carry on inspiring the design of new products, such as engines, transmissions, and chassis. For more than twenty years, Royce stayed away from Derby. He and

his entourage split their time between England's south coast (at West Wittering, in Sussex from 1919), and La Mimosa, a villa in Le Canadel on the Mediterranean coast of the French Riviera. According to the great automotive historian, Anthony Bird:

"But where Royce went, his work went with him, and though he lived in retirement for twenty years the volume and value of the work he inspired and directed are impressive by any standard."

It was not, and would never be, an indolent retirement, for Royce was the true inspiration behind new cars like the 20-horsepower, the Phantom I, and the Phantom II; the new six-cylinder engines; the world-beating R-Type and Merlin aircraft engines; and finally the automotive V-12 engine which was developed for use in the Phantom III.

In the meantime, the refinement, upgrading, and modernization of the Silver Ghost pedigree carried on. The engine was enlarged to 7,428 cc in 1909 raising peak power to about 60-horsepower, and increasing the low-speed torque. A new type of three-speed gearbox was installed at about the same time (with a reversion to four speeds in 1913-14), and cantilever rear leaf springs were used instead of platform rear spring suspension, beginning in 1908.

Nothing, though, was allowed to detract from the refinement, the manufacturing standards, and the individual attention to predelivery road testing and "debugging" that was always a feature of these cars.

Although high performance was never a "given" with these cars, before the outbreak of war, a series of fine Silver Ghost-based cars competed with honor in the Austrian Alpine Trial. These cars (sometimes known as "Continentals," but more familiarly as "Alpine Eagles") had up to 75 horsepower and rakish coachwork, which delivered a top speed of more than 80 miles per hour. James Radley's car won outright in 1913, and again in 1914, infuriating the Teutonic nations on their own doorstep.

When the Great War (later, of course, known as the First World War) erupted in August 1914, it took everyone but a few deep thinking British statesmen by surprise. Rolls-Royce, like other car makers, had made no preparations for a conflict that they had not seen coming, but they soon rallied to the cause.

The Silver Ghost chassis was soon made available, and pressed into service, not only for use in staff cars, ambulances, and tenders, but quite amazingly as armored cars too. Unless these armored cars had their tires machine gunned by the enemy, it seemed impossible to

immobilize them. In fact they were such a success that a few survivors were pressed into service more than twenty years later in World War too.

Rolls-Royce, however, soon concluded that aircraft engines would also be needed, and designed their own V-8 in short order, delivering power units to the British Royal Flying Corps before the end of 1915. This was just the start of an enterprise that would eventually come to dominate the company's workshops and balance sheet.

After the guns fell silent on November 11, 1918, it took time for industry to revert to peacetime operations. Companies like Rolls-Royce, whose products had been heavily involved on the ground and the air for the previous four years, could apply all manner of lessons to private cars. Not only was the Silver Ghost as popular as ever, but Rolls-Royce had plans to keep on improving it, notably by specifying a brake servo, and also by being one of the first British concerns to fit four-wheel brakes.

It was typical of Rolls-Royce that it had taken years

This was the engine bay, and fascia/instrument panel details of a U.S. built "Springfield" Phantom I. Owners were not expected to do their own maintenance in those days – that job was left to the chauffeur.

to assess the best features of all its rivals, so the chosen brake servo was a friction-operated disc device, operated from the gearbox, and one that leaned heavily on the previous experience of both Hispano-Suiza and Renault. There was no question of patent infringement, of course, for suitable license deals were negotiated and royalty payments agreed before the system could be standardized.

Although a U.S. built "Springfield" Rolls-Royce was always beautifully built, details such as the whitewall tires and the layout of the folding softtop usually indicated its origins.

This "Springfield" Phantom I had twin-blade front bumpers (note the extra "RR" badge in the center of the bars) and massive, high-mounted, headlamps.

The major thrust of the early postwar years, however, was to turn Rolls-Royce into a two-model concern, with the design and introduction of a new "small" model, the 20-horsepower, which went on sale in 1922. "Small," of course, needs explanation, for this was still a big, costly, and impressive 3,127 cc-engined machine (an overhead-valve six, with peak power output of 50 horsepower) – it was only small by comparison with the Silver Ghost, which still ruled the roost at Derby.

Because Rolls-Royce meant this to be more of an owner-driver machine than the Silver Ghost, the "Twenty" came complete with a three-speed gearbox, and centrally mounted gear and handbrake levers. To prove, though, that even great minds sometimes get things wrong, the clientele disliked what they saw, so a traditional right-hand change (with a right-hand brake lever) was adopted in 1925.

Although the Twenty was itself important, its new engine was a cornerstone of the company's future. Over the years, in every detail except one – the space between cylinder bore centers – this overhead valve six was enlarged, and made more robust, more powerful, and even more durable. Still in series production after more than thirty years, it finally topped out at 4,887 cc, with an (unstated, but widely known) output of 200 horsepower, linking the 1950s with the 1920s.

It was no wonder, therefore, when the technical chief, Harry Grylls, read a learned paper about this remarkable engine to the Institute of Mechanical Engineers in 1963, that he titled it "The History of a Dimension" – that dimension being the 4.150 inches between cylinder bores. As Grylls admitted, by the end of its life, this was the only feature linking the 1920s power unit with the 1950s descendant.

In the meantime, the company had set up shop in North America, where Silver Ghosts (and, later, Phantom Is) were manufactured in Springfield,

Massachusetts. Rolls-Royce did this by buying a disused factory from the American Wire Wheel Company, and starting up a new corporation with a capital in excess of $3 million.

It is important to stress that these cars were constructed with American-built components – very few chassis parts were regularly sent over the Atlantic from Derby. In the beginning, the U.S.-built cars would be almost identical to those being produced back in England, though a number of U.S.-sourced components were later added and, of course, the body shells were always sourced in America.

Although there were several good reasons for such an enterprise – which included getting around the high tariffs currently being imposed on imported cars and the availability of trained technicians who had been working on U.S.-built Rolls-Royce aircraft engines – the high ideals were never matched by the results.

One reason, perhaps, was that in the United States, in certain social circles there had always been a certain snob value to the purchase of an imported car, which rebounded on Rolls-Royce when those self-same cars were actually built "at home." Another, rectified within two years, was that all original "Springfield" Ghosts had right-hand steering, which was not ideal for cars being driven in the United States.

By 1924, LHD "Springfields" were being built with a three-speed gearbox, with central gear change and brake levers – all of which were more familiar to North American drivers. Body styles gradually but persistently became more obviously influenced by North American fashion. Silver Ghosts were produced there until 1926, after which the "New Phantom" (Phantom I, as it later became known) took over; the 20-horsepower model was never manufactured at Springfield.

Although manufacture and sales from Springfield continued steadily for ten years – before, into and through the worst of the Depression – Rolls-Royce closed down the enterprise in 1931 before sales dried up completely. All in all, there were 1,701 "Springfield" Silver Ghosts, and 1,225 "Springfield" Phantom Is – which equated to an average of almost 300 cars a year. The best year was 1928, when 400 cars were produced – then, a year later, Wall Street crashed, and production declined to a mere 100 cars in 1930.

Peanuts, you might say, but at that time this compared with an average Derby output of between 800 and 900 cars a year. Springfield, therefore, was making one-third of the number of cars being produced at Derby, but was serving just one market.

In America, however, it would be many years before any other European car maker tried to take up the same sort of challenge, which makes the company's original enterprise look very brave indeed.

At home, in the meantime, there was steady progress. In 1925 the long-running Silver Ghost was finally discontinued, to be replaced by a car originally called the new Phantom; as two further generations of Phantom followed during the 1930s, this car was eventually better known as the Phantom I.

In fairness, there was rather less to the New Phantom than meets the eye, for the long-established Silver Ghost chassis was retained, but this time powered by a brand new overhead-valve six-cylinder engine of 7,668 cc. Because Rolls-Royce had already decided that discretion and an air of mystery would add to their reputation for dignity above all, peak power outputs were no longer quoted. Behind the curtain, as it were, it was known that the new "six" produced between 80 and 90 horsepower, slightly more on later cars when an aluminum cylinder head was fitted. Ultimate performance was not thought important, but silence and refinement certainly were –

While the 40/50hp "Silver Ghost" was on its way to maturity in the 1910s and early 1920s, body styles were impressive rather than elegant, conventional rather than startling. Until 1922, when the new Twenty arrived, it was the only model in this patrician range.

and both were delivered in abundance.

Although body styles, as produced by magnificent independent coachbuilders like H.J. Mulliner, Hooper, and Barker, continued to change gradually, though from one year to the next there would only be subtle alterations to wing profiles, cabin proportions and fittings. Many Rolls-Royce cars of this period were still produced with formal limousine coachwork (there was still a big demand for Rolls-Royce trained, and approved, chauffeurs), though increasing numbers of "owner-driver" machines were also being commissioned, some of them with positively rakish drop-top styles.

Technically, though, the big leap forward occurred in 1929, when both models were replaced and updated. Not only did the Twenty, which had enjoyed a seven-year career during which 2,940 cars were built, give way to the 3,699 cc-engined 20/25-horsepower, but the new Phantom retired after only four years, in favor of the Phantom II. Both cars had new, more rigid and more conventional chassis layouts, but remained conventional in almost every mechanical detail, for

neither Henry Royce nor his management team saw any need to gamble on advanced (and, in their eyes, unproven) engineering when they could concentrate on producing the best possible cars of an existing level.

Their performance, was neither outstanding nor disappointing. A Phantom II could be relied upon to cruise at more than 60 miles per hour, and to top out at 80 miles per hour or more, while a 20/25-horsepower was more sedate, with a flat-out maximum of 65–70 miles per hour. Because these cars did not have power-assisted steering (no such mechanism existed at the time), driving, particularly at low speeds, could be hard work. A Phantom II could weigh well over 5,000 pounds, even more if extra bulky coachwork was chosen.

If you had to ask about the likely fuel consumption of either car (it could be as awful as 8 miles per gallon on Phantom IIs), it probably meant that you could not afford to run such a patrician car in any case. All the cars had four-speed transmissions with a right-hand gear change on right-hand-drive cars, while four-wheel brakes with the friction-type servo mechanism were now an established part of the specification.

Thus reequipped, Rolls-Royce was as ready as any other maker of luxury cars to face the future, but everything wasn't going their way. By 1930, with sales tending to melt away because of the Depression, which was spreading across the world, and with car-buying tycoons running for cover, Rolls-Royce was increasingly worried about its competitors. In Europe, Daimler, Hispano-Suiza, and Lanchester were all threats, but what now thoroughly alarmed the company was the growing challenge from Bentley.

As will be made clear in Chapter 2, during the 1920s, Bentley's out-and-out sports cars had steadily evolved into big, comfortable, fast, and desirable touring cars and, in 1930, the very accomplished six-cylinder 8-liter chassis had appeared, really as a head-to-head competitor to the latest Phantom II. Not only was the 8-liter just as costly, and just as noble looking as the Rolls-Royce, but it was also much faster.

In the short term, Rolls-Royce could do no more than push through Phantom II improvements, but suddenly, in June 1931, there appeared to be an opportunity. As detailed in the next Chapter, when a finance house called in its loans, Bentley dived into receivership. But an undercover agent of Rolls-Royce bought the business after a tense boardroom battle, and the threat from Bentley was neutralized. Instead of competing with the 8-liter Bentley, Rolls-Royce could kill it off – which it did very rapidly.

In the "vintage" period, Rolls-Royce styles were impressive rather than beautiful, but the equipment and finish of tourers like this "Silver Ghost" were always impeccable.

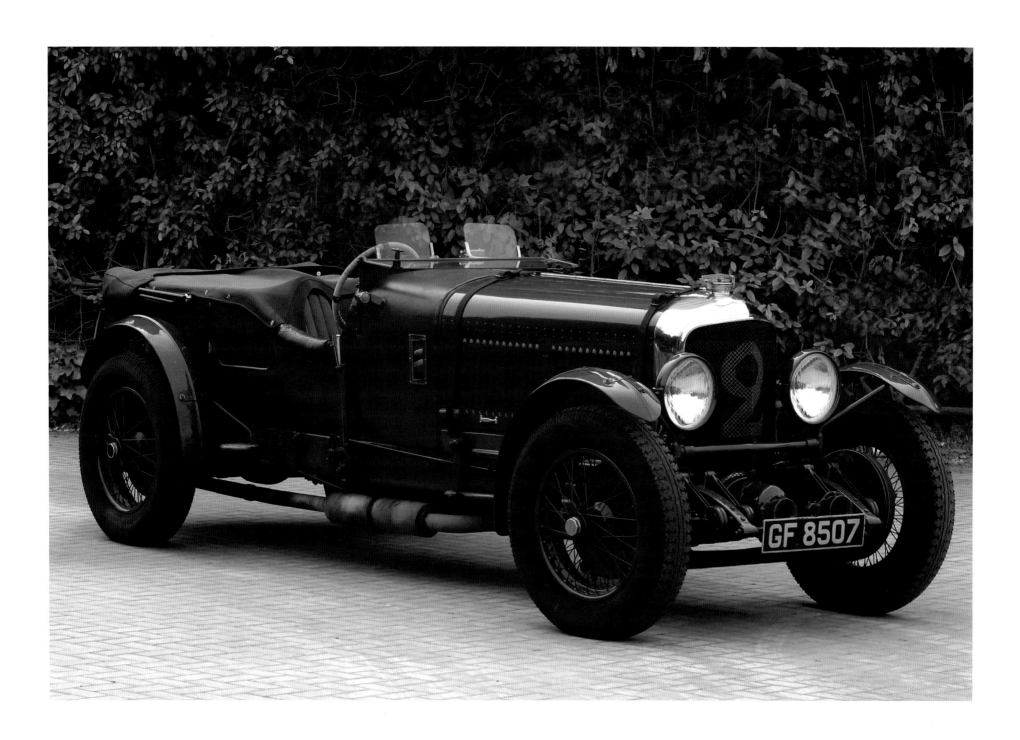

THE VINTAGE BENTLEY

A NEW SPORTING BRAND

ROLLS-ROYCE'S FUTURE PARTNER, BENTLEY, CAME ONTO THE SCENE nearly two decades after Henry Royce had set up shop in Manchester, England. Royce's workshops had already been open for four years before Walter Owen Bentley, born in 1888 in London, came onto the scene. By the time Bentley Motors was established, Rolls-Royce was already famous as a builder of top-class cars (the Silver Ghost) and of aircraft engines.

Like Royce, Bentley himself took time to get involved
in automobiles and, in fact did not ride in a car at all
until he had left school. After completing more formal
education than Royce ever had – he attended Clifton
College, in Bristol, England, until he was 16 years old –
he also entered Britain's proud railway industry, as a
premium apprentice at the Great Northern Railway
workshops in Doncaster. This meant that his parents
had to pay for the privilege of seeing him learn a trade,
a long process that took a full five years.

Although he was well briefed in basic engineering
principles when he came out of Doncaster, Bentley did
not warm to the idea of working in that industry for a
living. In 1910, he turned to motorcycles and cars, and
dabbled in motor racing at Brooklands, before finding a
job with the National Motor Cab Company of
London. From there he and his brother, H.M. Bentley,
moved into the motor trade, started importing cars like
the French D.F.P. marque, and got involved in more
modern engineering, notably in the evolution of light-
alloy pistons.

The excellence of his pistons, incidentally, provided
an early link with Rolls-Royce. In 1914 he was invited to
Derby to meet the team that was working on the Renault
aircraft engine, and on the design of the original Rolls-

The 'works' 3-Liter Bentley, already damaged after its now-legendary multi-car smash at White House corner in the 1927 Le Mans race, being refuelled in the pits later in the race.

Royce Eagle engine which was to follow it.

With the outbreak of World War I, Bentley joined
the Royal Navy Voluntary Reserve (RNVR), but soon
gravitated to engineering work with the navy and with
aircraft engines. Work on those engines soon took up
most of his time, and in due course he formulated the
design of his own engine, the BR1, an air-cooled rotary

unit inspired as a great improvement on the existing
French Clerget unit. The long arm of coincidence then
set in, for Bentley was directed to Humber Limited of
Coventry, England, to see those engines finalized and
put in to production. There he met F.T. "Monkey"
Burgess, who was already established as a designer of
racing sports cars. When peace arrived in 1918, the two

were already firm friends.

After the war, W.O. Bentley was awarded some $32,800 by the authorities as an award for his work on military engines. The Income Tax authorities eventually allowed this to go through without taking their rapacious share, and the idea of making Bentley motorcars soon took root. With this money, and that of other hopeful investors, Bentley Motors was set up in London in 1919. F.T. Burgess was to be the chief designer, and Bentley himself the managing director, the inspiration, and the figurehead.

On rather similar lines to the Vauxhall 30/98, which had already appeared before the war, the original Bentley was to be a solid, no-nonsense sports car. Its engine was to be a totally new 3-liter four-cylinder unit, which would have a single overhead camshaft and four valves per cylinder.

That layout, incidentally, was modern but by no means unique, for previous users had included Mercedes, an example of whose 1914 Grand Prix engine had somehow come to be interned in London after the outbreak of World War I. A friend of a friend had told W.O. Bentley this engine, which was tucked away in Mercedes' Long Acre showrooms in central London. "W.O." liberated the engine, and delivered it

When Bentley decided to celebrate the 1927 Le Mans victory with a dinner at London's Savoy Hotel, the only way that the car could be squeezed in through the doors was by removing front and rear axles, and the fenders, then reassembling the machine indoors.

Although this 4 1/2-liter Bentley retains most of the correct running gear, its wheels and tyres are of a later, 1930s, type, while the body shell itself is a replacement with more flowing lines, probably dating from the mid- to late-1930s.

to Rolls-Royce for their study, but took good care to learn everything that he could along the way.

Design work began in Conduit Street, London, an address that would later become firmly linked with Rolls-Royce. The very first engine burst into life on a test bed in the D.F.P. service station in New Street Mews, not far from London's Regent's Park, in October 1919. The matron of a local hospital immediately turned up to complain about the racket, and future work had to be done elsewhere.

Although the first prototype car was completed and shown before the end of 1919, the new "3-liter" car was not yet ready for sale. Neither of the West End premises Bentley was then using, was at all suitable for automobile manufacture, so the search for new quarters began in earnest.

A site was eventually found in Oxgate Lane, Cricklewood, on the northernmost outskirts of London. Brand new, but very simply equipped, at the time, this building was adequate for Bentley's ambitions, but could never have been expanded to allow the company to become a major manufacturer. Accordingly, it would be speedily abandoned by Rolls-Royce after the takeover in 1931, and was quickly sold.

The arrival of Bentley, as a new marque, was greeted

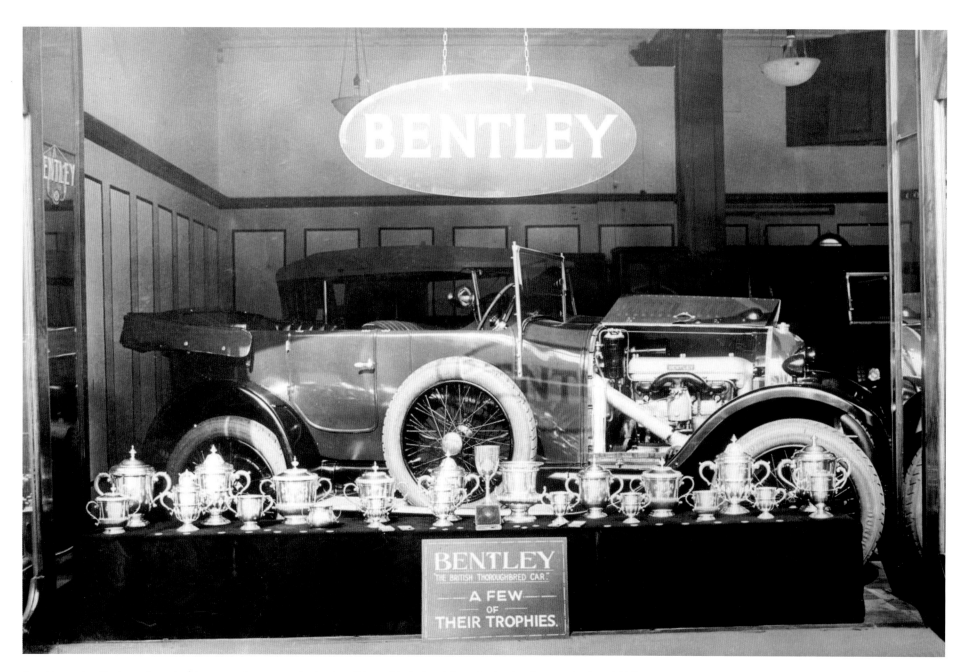

From time to time, Bentley made much of its motor racing successes, by showing off its trophies in the window of its London showrooms in the mid-1920s.

Although the "Blower" Bentley 4½-liter was a fine-looking sports car, it was effectively a private enterprise model, inspired by race driver Sir Henry Birkin, for W.O. Bentley himself did not approve of supercharging. Only fifty such road cars, and five special racers, were produced.

the business was greatly reduced.

In ten years, between 1921 and 1931, when the financial house of cards collapsed yet again, there would be six distinctly different Bentley models offered on a multitude of different wheelbase lengths. Four-cylinder and six-cylinder engines ranged from the 3-liters to (finally) 8-liters, there being common DNA but a multitude of detail differences between the various types.

At this time, very wisely, Bentley (like Rolls-Royce) wanted nothing to do with the building of bodies. Every machine was sold as a rolling chassis, after which a customer was directed to one of a group of favored coachbuilders who would complete the machine. It was no coincidence that one of the most favored of all body suppliers was Vanden Plas, whose premises were only a mile or two away. Not only would Vanden Plas produce hundreds of body shells, but they would be intimately involved with the racing program that followed.

From 1921, when the first 3-liter model was delivered, until the early 1930s, when the last of the 8-liter types crept unhappily out of the doors of the dying concern, the essence of every vintage Bentley was passed down from model to model, and was there for all to see. Every car was built up around a rock-solid

warmly, and the cars themselves delivered more than their mere specification promised. However, for the next ten years, the problem was not to sell the cars or to design new ones, but to make profits with which to keep the business afloat. W.O. himself seemed to be above such sordid details or, in truth, did not to understand enough about the subject. The fact is that the original heavily mortgaged business would have to be rescued by multimillionaire playboy/racedriver Woof Barnato in 1926, after which W.O.'s own share in

By the end of the 1920s, Bentley was by far the most successful British marque in sports car racing. Here, two of the "works" Speed Six models race around the concrete bowl at Brooklands, in Surrey, England.

In 1920, Bentley set up a new factory in Cricklewood, London, to build its cars. Equipment was very sparse in the early days, but every new car was road tested before being delivered.

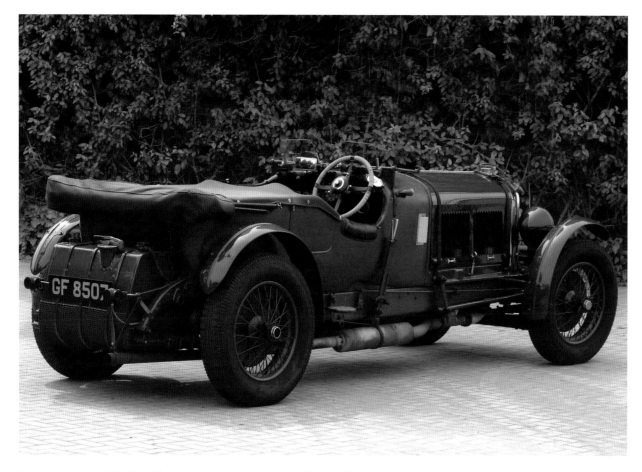

Two views of a late-1920s Speed Six, with four-seater open tourer coachwork. That is a long hood, and it was almost full of engine!

separate chassis frame, which had deep channel-section side members. All but one model (the last, the 4-liter) had an overhead-camshaft engine with four valves per cylinder. All had four-speed nonsynchronized gearboxes separated from the engine, operated by the usual type of right-hand gear shift, which was fashionable at this time.

Before going into detail of the cars themselves, we must keep on reminding ourselves just how rare and exclusive every "vintage" Bentley of the 1921-1931 period actually was. Although big items like chassis frames were pressed out, and supplied by outside contractors, much of the rest of the chassis took shape

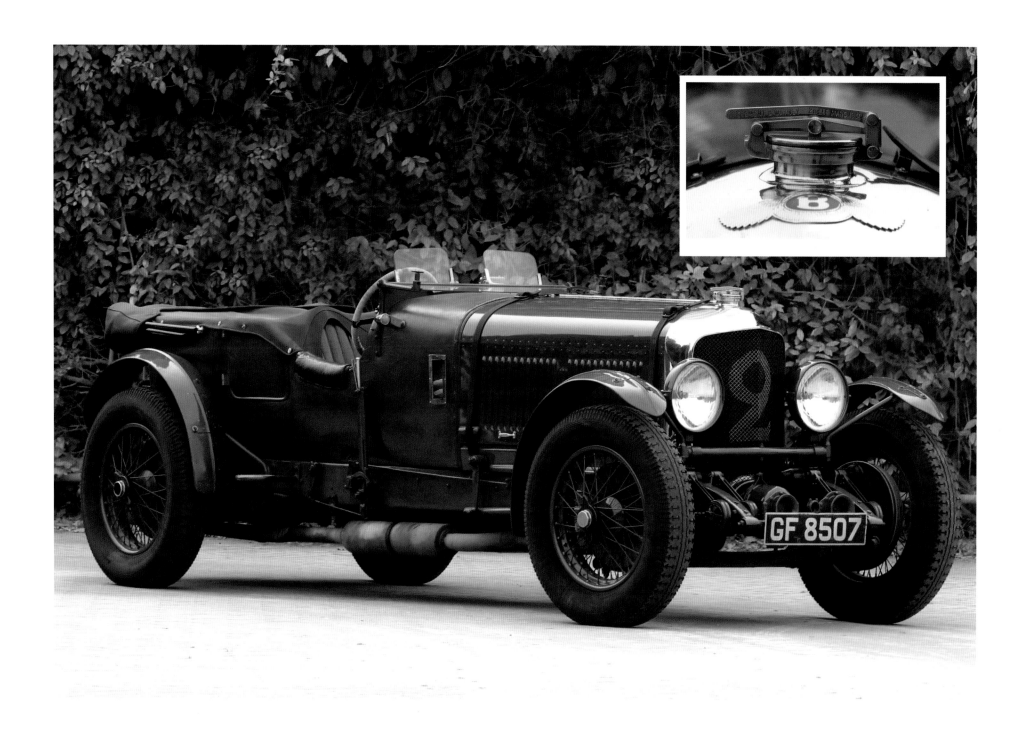

The fuel tank (left) of a Speed Six was exposed, but usually protected from flying stones, while the engine (below) was an impressive straight six.

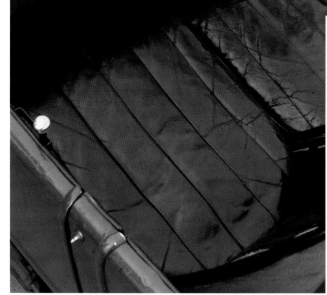

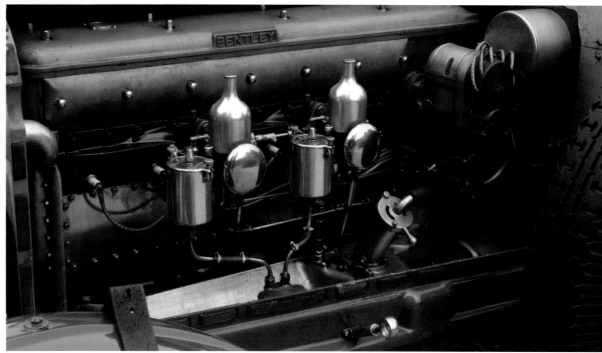

Left: One of the most popular of all "vintage" Bentleys was the 6½-liter Speed Six. Although many were supplied with closed coachwork, the most memorable were four-seater tourers like this, with a Vanden Plas body shell.

slowly, methodically, and with great care inside the simple brick sheds which soon filled out the Cricklewood site.

Production and sales built up together. But on average over the period, annual production of Bentleys was only about 300 cars, which meant that Cricklewood was rarely shipping out more than six or seven chassis in a week. It took much financial juggling, and a great deal of special pleading with some suppliers, to make sure that Bentley's erratic cash flow could be massaged to keep the business afloat.

This helps to explain, too, why so much of a 1920s Bentley was handcrafted, for at this tiny rate of production there was no justification to provide mechanization and tooling for series manufacture. Even so, engines and gearboxes were always manufactured to demandingly high standards, and every one was tested thoroughly before it was released for fitting to a new chassis. It was not for many years (and following huge improvements in the standard of available fuels) that enthusiasts discovered how much extra power could be extracted from these remarkable power units without blowing them up. A number of them were supercharged, and delivered phenomenal horsepower and steam engine-like torque.

Not only were all of these Bentleys bodied by independent coachbuilders, but each car was extensively road tested on the public highway before going off for completion. Bentley, like Rolls-Royce, completed a fully operational rolling chassis, complete with the front radiator, the hood panels, and the firewall, but the rest of the car was settled between the customer and his coachbuilder.

In the case of the most noteworthy coachbuilders – such as Vanden Plas, who provided bodies for 669 cars in ten years, and Gurney Nutting (360 in a similar period) – coachbuilders developed standardized designs, which were, and remain, instantly recognizable to latter-day enthusiasts.

On the other hand, in those ten years, no fewer than 120 coachbuilders (mostly British, but also European) supplied bodies of one sort or another, and in some cases it was only the radiator block itself (which Bentley insisted should be retained) that linked one type with another. Although Bentley left the choice of bodywork to its client, it insisted on inspecting, and approving, the ensemble, before confirming the lengthy warranty that applied to all of these cars.

Incidentally, although many of the most golden Bentley memories seem to feature sports cars and

racing, a fair proportion of all cars built actually had sedan car shells. Once the six-cylinder chassis became available, more and more closed Bentleys were built, some of them being limousines, rather rakishly styled. It was this trend, more than any other, that alarmed Rolls-Royce in the end.

The life and times of the independent Bentley concern can be summed up, brutally, in just a few paragraphs. The 3-liter was the original model, and the stalwart of this family of cars – more than half of Cricklewood's ten-year output was of 3-liter models – but it was the six-cylinder $6^1/2$-liter which followed, that truly cemented the marque's reputation.

Whereas the 3-liter was a lively sports car, the $6^1/2$-liter was truly fast, and could be outpaced by few of its rivals, and by none of them in as much comfort and with such aplomb. It was all very well, critics suggested, buying a latter-day six-cylinder Mercedes-Benz, if it could only be made to go faster by bringing the optional supercharger into action. And what good was that, they asked, if the engine noise was awful, the reliability fell away, and Mercedes-Benz would not approve of its continual use?

Preparing for the launch of a new six-cylinder engine absorbed most of Bentley's scanty financial

Bentley Chairman's famous "Blue Train beating" Speed Six featured rakish Gurney Nutting coachwork This car could easily reach 100 miles per hour, a phenomenal speed for 1930, when this car beat the famous French train from the Mediterranean to the English Channel.

racing program now feeding huge publicity bonuses into the company, all looked well for years to come.

Which it was, until the Wall Street crash of 1929 began to affect trade in Europe, and a European-wide depression swiftly set in. The 8-liter was a great car, but was far too expensive to sell in big numbers, and was no longer salable to impoverished sportsmen. Against W.O.'s wishes, his company then went on to produce the 4-liter in 1931. Although this car had a good engine, which was much cheaper to build that the earlier types, it was not a Bentley in-house design, and the founder would have nothing to do with it. Instead, the 4-liter was really a finance man's idea of how costs could be reduced without losing performance or looks – and was meant to produce a more suitable chassis for use by the carriage trade.

By this time, the Bentley company was working on yet another source of working capital. By 1926 the company's original funds were quite exhausted, for profits were not always being made, and mortgages that had been taken out on the factory buildings could no longer be serviced. W.O himself had approached Woolf Barnato before the end of 1925. Eventually the original company's shares were written down, the old company wound up (in June 1926). A new Bentley Motors

capital, but the result was a masterpiece. Not only was the 6½-liter a fine car, but its descendants, the more powerful and even more sporting Speed Six and the luxurious and magnificent 8-liter, were further improved, yet more capable, and even more legendary.

The 4½-liter, which arrived in 1927, was the nominated successor to the 3-liter, this time with an engine using features of the original "four" and the later "six", though the changeover was not immediate. With such cars on sale, and with a glitteringly successful

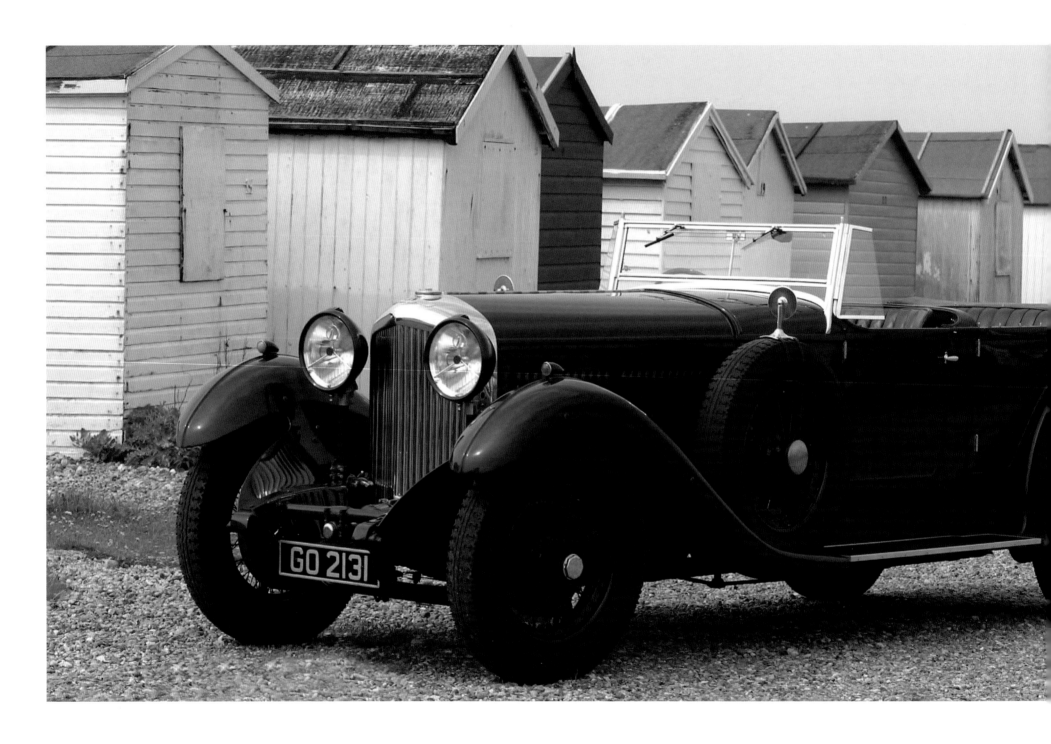

Like other "vintage" Bentleys, this 8-liter – a late model in the Cricklewood scheme of things – shared details with other cars in the range. This particular engine had twin SU carburettors. Two spare wheels were carried – one on each side of the bodywork.

Those were the days in which rear seat passengers had a good deal of space, when the gear shift lever was on the right of the driver's seat, and when (nice touch, this) there was a letter "B" cast into the cap that the mechanic removed to add oil.

All Bentleys were large, but some were even more impressively bulky than others. This enormous 8-liter model carries typical four-door open tourer bodywork of the period. In spite of its bulk, such a car could easily reach 100 miles per hour – an astonishing speed for the 1930 period

Limited was formed with a working capital of $7 million, and the new chairman was Barnato himself, as the controlling shareholder.

W.O. Bentley was shifted smartly sideways in these maneuvers. At first, he was designated managing director, but after May 1927 he was only jointly in charge, in unwilling harness with the Marquis de Casa Maury (a Cuban banker, who was a friend of Barnato). Before long, though, even that uneasy situation was dissolved, for W.O. lost his title, and ended up running

These are details so typical of the last of the huge and prestigious "Cricklewood" Bentleys of the late 1920s and early 1930s. Engine controls, operating on quadrants, were located on the steering wheel boss, and the six-cylinder overhead camshaft engine (this is an 8-liter) dominated a crowded engine bay.

the racing team and merely advising on the technical programs still going ahead.

In later years, W.O. Bentley went on record as saying that he hated the very idea of cars like the $4^1/2$-liter "Blower," and the 4-liter models, which were both put on sale against his wishes. Tragically and unhappily, his personal control of his own company, and the cars that were his babies, had lasted for only seven years. On the

other hand, he cannot be blamed in the slightest, for the financial crash that came in 1931.

It would be too easy to let the merits of each Bentley car be obscured by the political and financial machinations that occupied the 1926 – 1931 period, but this must certainly not be the case here.

It was the original Bentley road car, the charismatic 3-liter, that set the tone for the period, and the long-

stroke four-cylinder engine that set it apart from its rivals. Having studied all the rivals and learned what they could from the aviation industry, W.O.'s team produced a sturdy power unit with its cylinder block and heads cast in one unit, and its single overhead camshaft driven by a shaft and gears from the nose of the crank shaft. The original power output was reputedly 80 horsepower (though such figures were not publicized at the time), which helped push the 3-liter along at up to 80 miles per hour.

The gearbox was mounted separately and was operated by a lever to the right of the driver (outside the coachwork in some cases), and the brakes (rear wheel only at first) were cable operated – all at an original cost (rolling chassis only) of more than $4,000, which made the car one of Britain's mot expensive sports cars.

Several different wheelbase lengths were available during the eight years that the 3-liter was on sale (the longest, suitable for closed coachwork, was 130.5 inches long). Four-wheel brakes were standard from 1923, and from 1928, a number of later model $4^1/2$-liter components were fitted. Naturally, sales fell away after more modern Bentleys were introduced, but no fewer than 1,622 3-liters of all types were eventually sold. This was undoubtedly helped along by the company's fine racing record – for 3-liters won the prestigious Le Mans 24 Hour race in 1924 and again in 1927.

The $6^1/2$-liter first appeared in 1925, and though superficially it looked like the 3-liter (coachbuilders sometimes adapted existing body styles from one model to the next) it was really a new design. It was built on a more robust chassis with a choice of much longer

wheelbases (that eventually ranged from 132 inches to a gargantuan 152.5 inches). Power was by a magisterial overhead-camshaft six-cylinder engine of 6,597 cc. Different in many technical ways from the four and was not, by any means, a four with extra cylinders tacked on. Bentley's fixed-head six drove its camshaft by a wonderfully complex cluster of three connecting rods and eccentrics. This was an arrangement that W.O. must surely have seen on steam locomotives when he was an apprentice in Doncaster.

Even in its original form, this magnificent engine pushed out up to 147 horsepower, and even with large and spacious coachwork a $6^1/2$-liter could beat 90 miles per hour. High geared, effortless, impressive – and incredibly expensive at nearly $6,000 for the chassis only (which meant nearly $8,200 for a complete car) the $6^1/2$-liter was a much-loved machine. Like the 180 horsepower Speed Six, which followed the $6^1/2$-liter in 1929, it was a car that made Rolls-Royce sit up and think. The Speed Six was also a successful race car, for "works" machines won the Le Mans 24 Hour race in 1929 and again in 1930. The last victory was so crushing that the team was immediately disbanded, as it had no more points to make. In five years, just 545 cars (181 of them Speed Sixes) were built.

After the launch of the $6^1/2$-liter, the mixing and matching began. Introduced in 1927, the $4^1/2$-liter was at once a replacement for the 3-liter, but the car was also related to the $6^1/2$-liter model. Almost every $4^1/2$-liter was built on the longer (130.5-inch) wheelbase first seen in the 3-liter. The styles looked remarkably similar, but this time the engine was an amalgam of new and old types. It shared the same bore and stroke as the $6^1/2$-liter (100mm x 140mm), but retained the shaft-and-helical-gear camshaft drive of the 3-liter. Because the cars were tending to get larger and heavier, this new engine was needed to maintain performance. With 100 – 105 horsepower and a lot of torque (one enthusiastic buyer who loved these cars described the $4^1/2$-liter as having a "great bloody thump"), this was a car that sold steadily until the end. With just one Le Mans victory to its credit (in 1928) 665 of all types were built in four years.

The $4^1/2$-liter "Blower" followed in 1929. ("Blower" refers to the use of a Villiers supercharger, which was mounted up front ahead of the radiator shell, between the front of the chassis rails). It might have looked glamorous to the outside, but was a real cuckoo in the nest. Racing driver Sir Henry ("Tim") Birkin was its cheerleader, for he wanted even more powerful Bentleys to go racing with, but W.O himself disliked supercharging and would have nothing to do with it.

In the end, chairman Woolf Barnato, himself a racing driver, authorized the production of the fifty cars needed to get the "Blower" approved for use in racing. Birkin's team was sponsored by the Hon. Dorothy Paget, and located at Welwyn in Hertfordshire, England. The new 175 horsepower engined car was put on sale.

There was good news and bad news. Because the 100-mile per hour road cars cost only about $400 more than the normal $4\frac{1}{2}$-liter in chassis form - $4,700 instead of $4,300 – the fifty-car requirement was easily met. Birkin's racing program, though, was not at all successful, and in fact, he never managed a victory in his special "Blowers." Highlights included second place in the free-formula French Grand Prix, and the building of a race-winning special single-seater, which spent much of its career racing around the concrete bowl at Brooklands.

By any standards, the "vintage" Bentley reached its climax in 1930, when the $6\frac{1}{2}$-liter model grew up even further, with a brand new and rock-solid chassis, and an enlarged engine – this was the legendary 8-liter. Chassis with a choice of 144 inches or 156 inches were available. The 7,983 cc, six-cylinder engine produced an estimated 200 – 225 horsepower, and even when equipped with the impressive closed bodies being chosen by most customers, this was a genuine 100-mile per hour car. Not only did an 8-liter look magnificent, but at almost $7,600 for the chassis (perhaps $10,000-plus for a complete machine), it was a head-to-head competitor for the latest Rolls-Royce Phantom II.

Huge, expensive, and only bought by the lucky few, of whom there were dwindling numbers, the 8-liter struggled to make its mark, and must have contributed to Bentley's financial downfall. More than thirty-three of the original sanction of 100 chassis had to be sold after the company called in the receiver.

Even so, these were magnificent machines, and have almost all have survived into the present. Many of them have been rebodied with sporting bodies rather than the sedans or limousines with which they were originally equipped.

The last of the Cricklewood Bentleys was another car of which W.O. did not approve. The other directors, effectively Barnato nominees, wanted to get cost and complicated design out of the $4\frac{1}{2}$-liter, and equip it with a six-cylinder engine. The result was the 4-liter, which had a unique type of six-cylinder engine with only two valves per cylinder. It was the only Cricklewood Bentley to have a detachable cylinder head, the head encasing overhead intake valves, with side valves in the cylinder block itself.

Postwar Rolls-Royces and Bentleys would both use such a system, but in 1931 this engine was engineered with advice from outside consultants (both Harry Ricardo and Harry Weslake were involved at one time or another) and W.O hated the very sight of it.

Perhaps the Not-Invented-Here syndrome applied, for there is no doubt that the 4-litre engine delivered the goods, even though it had to drive an over-engineered chassis, which was a shortened version of that used in the 8-liter. Four-liter engines produced 120 horsepower, significantly more than the $4\frac{1}{2}$-liter ever had, and smoothness was a bonus.

Even so, because the 4-liter was launched in May 1931, just one month before the receiver was called in, it never really had a chance to establish itself. No more than a handful of these cars were ordered before the roof fell in, and it was not until mid-1932 that the fiftieth and last car was ordered.

In the meantime, Bentley's high profile racing program had blossomed, peaked, and fallen away. Operating profits were still hard to find, and the brutal truth is that Chairman Woolf Barnato was spending much less time at his Bentley business than he should have. After the Depression deepened in the 1930s, "vintage" Bentley sales slowed down so much that a financial collapse was almost inevitable, and it duly came in June 1931. This was the point at which the London Life Association Ltd., an insurance company that had made a large loan to Bentley, called in that loan when it was due, only to discover that Chairman Barnato, who held all the purse strings, was unwilling to pay them off.

With the motor racing program now at an end, Barnato, it was suggested, had tired of his loss-making "investment," and wanted rid of it. The playboy, it was said, wanted new toys to play with. Indeed, it was Barnato who appointed a receiver, and from that moment the original Bentley brand was doomed.

Even at that stage, a solution seemed to be possible, for the Napier firm of West London, who had built a series of fine cars up until the mid-1920s, wanted to get back into the automotive business. To start, they attracted W.O. Bentley to work for them, then set about persuading Receiver Patrick Frere that they should be allowed to gather up the wreckage of the company.

Unknown to Napier, however, Rolls-Royce had its own ambitions, and resolved to do the same, through a shadowy intermediary known as the British Central Equitable Trust (BCET). Matters came to a head in a courtroom in November 1931. Immediately after Napier had tabled an offer of $425,000, the BCET told the judge that they were empowered to offer more. A startled Napier company hastily conferred with their counsel, and offered $428,000. The judge brusquely told Napier that he was not an auctioneer, and that at 4:30 p.m. on the same day he would accept sealed bids, and that no more bargaining would be acceptable.

When the bids were opened up, the BCET was seen to have offered $515,000, and Bentley was knocked down to them. Napier's bid was dead in the water, W.O. was once again out of a job, and within days it became clear that the BCET was no more than a front organization for Rolls-Royce.

After only ten years, W.O. Bentley's dream was finally over. Even though he had been marginalized since the late 1920s, he had still kept control of his beloved racing team, and continued to influence some technical development in the company. But the financial realities had taken all precedence – and now it was up to Rolls-Royce to revive the brand.

Looking back, it is easy to see that these Bentleys were right for their time – but that by 1931 that time had gone. Rebirth would follow two years later, under the new ownership, with an entirely different type of automobile.

CHAPTER *Three*

MERGED IN THE 1930S

ROLLS-ROYCE AND BENTLEY TOGETHER

WHEN ROLLS-ROYCE TOOK OVER BENTLEY AT THE END OF 1931, it had to set out a new and more wide-ranging marketing strategy for the future. At that moment, four different models were on the market:

MODEL	ENGINE (cc)	CHASSIS PRICE (U.S.)
Rolls-Royce 20/25hp	3,669 cc	$4,305
Bentley 4-Liter	3,915 cc	$5,022
Rolls-Royce 40/50hp Phantom II	7,668 cc	$7,175
Bentley 8-Liter	7,983 cc	$7,585

Fortunately, in 1931-1932, Rolls-Royce was already quite content with its own current models – the 20/25hp and (40/50hp) Phantom II – for those had both been in production for two years, and had a proud reputation. Body styles (all of them still coming from separate coachbuilders) were gradually, but perceptibly, becoming less upright, with more sweeping lines, though not with any sign of going florid and flamboyant like those of their rivals from Europe and North America.

Technically, a whole series of detail changes were being phased into those cars as soon as they were ready. Synchromesh gearboxes (pioneered on General Motors cars a few years earlier), appeared on the 20/25, then, a year later, on the Phantom II. Complete centralized chassis lubrication arrived in the same period, as did hydraulic instead of friction shock absorbers.

Not that the vast majority of customers even knew about such details, though their chauffeurs most certainly did. Those were still the days in which a Rolls-Royce was to own, and to be driven in, but not actually to drive oneself. The chauffeur invariably lived close to the "big house" (often in an apartment alongside, or even on top of, the garage), and would have been responsible for keeping the cars immaculately clean, serviced, and in good repair.

Toward the end of his life, in the early 1930s, Sir Henry Royce (seated) inspired a youthful engineer, Ivan Evernden (standing) to interpret many of his technical ideas. Sir Henry died in 1933, but Evernden's influence continued at Rolls-Royce until the 1950s.

Modern marketing gurus would call this a misbalanced range, for the models were all crowded into a combined range that would only sell less than a thousand cars in a year. The planners were faced with selling four models, each with its own different chassis, and each with its own very different engine.

Not even for Rolls-Royce, where high prices, high build quality, and a peerless reputation all allowed the company to float above the general trade depression, could this situation continue. Even so, it was not until 1933 that the company would be able to unveil its vision of the future.

For the time being, therefore, Rolls-Royce could concentrate on the Bentley business, which it had bought without ever setting foot inside the doors. They knew what they had bought, and what they had to overcome. On the credit side, there was a remarkable reputation, especially among sporting-minded motorists. On the debit side, there was an under-capitalized, heavily indebted business, which needed a complete overhaul to make it viable. Even so, it would take two years before Rolls-Royce was ready to introduce the first of the cars that were to become known as "Rolls-Bentleys."

In any case, early in 1932 it became clear that Rolls-Royce had certainly not purchased Bentley to make use of its engineering, but for its marketing reputation. This was a pity, but was perhaps inevitable. The Bentley 8-liter had already shown that it was a magnificent machine, with unparalleled performance. No other British car, not even an out-and-out sports machine, could reach 100 miles per hour – which was as much of a holy grail in 1930 as 200 miles per hour would be today. The virtually still-born 4-liter was a far better car than many W.O. fanatics would ever admit, but neither the 8-liter or the 4-liter, which were "vintage" to the core, appealed to Rolls-Royce.

Stories that Rolls-Royce was terrified of the capabilities of the 8-liter and made haste to kill it off, were never denied, though this was not done with an axe, but tidily and in a business-like manner. After the Rolls-Royce takeover had been formalized, there were many existing Bentley enthusiasts who hoped that production and development of their favorite cars would soon resume, but this never happened.

However, to squeeze every penny out of the remains of their loss-making, bankrupt purchase, Rolls-Royce saw to it that incomplete cars were finished off at Cricklewood, and then sold, and that commitments to suppliers were honored. Later in the 1930s they even arranged for a handful of cars, including some mid-1920s style 3-liters to be assembled from existing parts. But that was that.

Whatever Bentley might have had in mind for improving the 4-liter and 8-liter models was speedily suppressed. Many of the staff and most of the workforce were laid off. Because there was no redundancy legislation in those days, and because job prospects in the engineering industry were poor, this was not a happy time for what had been a very close-knit manufacturing team at Cricklewood.

Once the existing stock of old-style Bentleys had been completed and sold, the machinery had been stripped out, and spare parts relocated, the Cricklewood factory premises were sold off. They were eventually absorbed into the Smiths Instruments complex, which was nearby. Although Rolls-Royce was determined to revive Bentley, and to make it into the profitable business that had somehow confounded successive managements in the 1920s, they were determined to do it in Derby, alongside Rolls-Royce cars and close to the aircraft engine business, which was becoming ever more important to the company.

Although there was some debate about the type of new model which ought to be developed, Rolls-Royce was always determined that it should take shape around existing or still-being-developed Rolls-Royce technology and expertise. In fact, except for the use of the famous trademark, there would be absolutely no links between the final W.O. Bentleys – the 4-liter and 8-liter types, and the first-ever "Rolls-Bentley," the $3^{1}/_{2}$-liter.

Except in one respect. When the dust of the unsavory bankruptcy, takeover battle, and rather seedy purchase had settled. Bentley's founder, W.O. Bentley found himself in an awkward position. Just as he was ready to start afresh, with Napier, Rolls-Royce dropped a bombshell. As W.O. would write later:

"My service agreement with Bentley Motors, Rolls-Royce informed me, was still in force. I was not a free man to select my own future. I was, they made clear, part of the assets which they had purchased, together with all my office furniture, my medals and cups and trophies . . . ."

After a most unsatisfactory and unsympathetic interview with Sir Henry Royce, W.O. was based in London, answerable to Percy Northey, later becoming technical adviser to the managing director (Arthur Sidgreaves) and spent an unhappy four years on the staff. He never again became a director of the company, and felt increasingly marginalized. Once his contract expired, in mid-1935, he walked away, joined Lagonda, and proceeded to revive that small concern's engineering for the next decade.

By that time, too, Sir Henry Royce had also died. Although well cosseted, he had spent more than twenty restless years flitting between seaside houses in Sussex, and at Le Canadel in the South of France. Although Rolls-Royce motorcars and aircraft engines were designed by a very competent team, no major innovation was ever finalized without Sir Henry and his peripatetic design team. In the last few years, for example, they had worked on the new engine for the Rolls-Royce Phantom II; the R-Type aircraft engine

(which would power Britain's Schneider Trophy-winning seaplanes); the PV-12 aircraft engine (which matured into the fabulously success Merlin); and on the automotive products that would lead to the introduction of the very first "Rolls-Bentley."

Sir Henry died on April 22, 1933, and although Rolls-Royce insists that the change in the background color of the "RR" badge – it went from red to black at about the same time – was purely coincidental, it makes an appealing folk tale about the way this man was venerated by all his staff and colleagues.

After Sir Henry's death, Rolls-Royce became a more conventionally managed company, but did not change its policies for several years. Although the two marques carried more prestige than almost any other, production was always very limited by the high prices, and was likely to remain so. Even when the assembly halls at Derby were accommodating three different product lines – the Bentley 3^1/$_2$-liter, Rolls-Royce 20/25 and Rolls-Royce Phantom II – no more than 30 chassis a week ever rolled out of the doors. Such limited production was not deliberate, but then, (as later) there were natural limits as to how many people could afford such expensive new cars.

At this stage, Rolls-Royce never made any great

attempt to drive down its costs. (In any case, as the saying goes, "gentlemen never discuss money.") Such a process would not be initiated until the end of the 1930s, would be thought through deeply during World War II, and would not become apparent until 1946. In fact, the company's celebrated development chief, Ernest Hives (later Lord Hives and Chairman) commented about the cost of a new car from Derby:

"Everything in our cars could be made a little bit cheaper – and a bit worse . . . ."

As with the Rolls-Royce cars of the period, there was no such thing as a standard body style, for as in the 1920s, every Bentley built at Derby would have a fully functioning, rolling chassis, before being shipped out to its chosen coachbuilder for a body to be built upon it. Only a year after the 3^1/$_2$-liter had been introduced, no fewer than fourteen coachbuilders – Arnold, Barker, Cockshoot, Freestone & Webb, Hooper, Mann Egerton, Arthur Mulliner, H.J. Mulliner, Gurney Nutting, Park Ward, Rippon, Thrupp & Maberly, Vanden Plas and James Young – were building their own special bodies on this chassis.

Even so, though you may love the integrated design of the original Rolls-Bentley, the fact is that it took ages for Rolls-Royce to decide what to do with Bentley's

This elegant Sedanca Coupe style (where the soft top could be furled back to this midway position), was one of many to be found on the Bentley 3½-liter of 1933-1936. The top speed, in great comfort and style, was well into the 90s.

future. The new Bentley model was not revealed until October 1933, and first deliveries to private owners did not begin until early 1934.

This was not an easy birth. Should it be an out-and-out sports car (like the vintage models), a graceful but otherwise nonsporty range or something in between? Eventually, in a classic case of compromise, Rolls-Royce decided to mix-and-match its own assets, and invent a new type of Bentley, which they almost immediately dubbed "The Silent Sports Car."

In the beginning, there was a secret "small-Rolls-Royce" project, coded "Peregrine;" which was already in existence at Derby, but in difficulties at the prototype stage. Facing up to the Depression, Rolls-Royce was already toying with producing a new small model.

In the 1930s, every "Derby" Bentley had bodywork specially built by a coachbuilder. The basis of the body was often a wooden (sometimes steel or aluminum) skeleton, with pressed or hand-formed steel or aluminium panels attached to it. This was a typical four-door sports sedan of the period.

Though obviously related to the Rolls-Royce of the period, a 1930s "Derby" Bentley had a character all of its own, including a high-output version of the six-cylinder engine, and a specially equipped, more "sporty" dashboard layout.

It was the details of a "Derby" Bentley that made them so visually pleasing, such as the noble radiator, the "Flying B" radiator cap mascot, and the detail inscriptions on the wire wheel "spinners."

Compared with the existing 20/25 horsepower model – which had a 132-inch wheelbase and a 3.7-liter engine, "Peregrine" was smaller, with a 126-inch wheelbase, and a 70 horsepower, $2^{3}/4$-liter, six-cylinder engine. W.O. himself described it as "a very nice little car, carrying a rather dainty radiator . . . . with a good turn of speed," but it always looked too expensive to build, and was likely to be canceled.

Rolls-Royce then set about supercharging the engine, so that it now produced over 100 horsepower, but discovered that this power unit was blowing cylinder head gaskets on a regular basis. Months later, one of the test team then suggested a more practical solution – why not modify the existing Rolls-Royce 20/25 engine, somehow shoehorn it into a modified version of the Peregrine chassis, then call it a Bentley?

According to historian Michael Frostick:

"It would be unfair to call it a committee car, for what they did, as Robotham has pointed out, was the obvious thing and not the work of genius. It did, however, produce a very pleasant car."

Except for using an updated version of the famous Bentley radiator and badge, the very first "Rolls-Bentley," therefore, had virtually no Bentley DNA in it at all, for Rolls-Royce engineer W.A. Robotham led the design team. This same strategy, incidentally, would be followed in the early 2000s, for the first VW-inspired Bentley – the Continental GT – which had even fewer traditional links with its illustrious past.

In other words, from 1933 to 1939, although what became affectionately known as "Derby" Bentleys, or "Rolls-Bentleys were supposedly different from the Rolls-Royces of the period (and Rolls-Royce liked to foster that myth), they were actually engineered by that company. They also shared major basic components (engines and transmissions – or "building blocks" as they would have been called later in the century) with the smaller Rolls-Royce models. But more importantly perhaps, the two marques still matched up to the other make's standards.

Even so, a Bentley 3$\frac{1}{2}$-liter was definitely not just a "badge-engineered" Rolls-Royce. In 1934, for instance, the 3$\frac{1}{2}$-liter was being built alongside the Rolls-Royce 20/25, yet the two cars had completely different chassis frames. The two engines had totally different cylinder heads (the Bentley had a hypoid bevel rear axle while the 20/25 was spiral bevel), and, of course, the Bentley used totally different, and far more sporting, body styles.

The difference, of course, was not merely in engineering and style, but in character. At a time when Rolls-Royce was certain that it was building "The Best Car in The World," they began to market the new Bentley as the "The Silent Sports Car." Brilliant! At one and the same time, it distanced the new Bentley from Rolls-Royce, and also from the earlier generation of Bentleys which it replaced.

The "Rolls-Bentleys" certainly seemed to appeal to an entirely different clientele from those who had bought vintage (or W.O.) Bentleys, and if phrases like "focus groups," or "marketing surveys" had even been invented at the time, Rolls-Royce would certainly have

From 1936 the "Rolls-Bentley" was enlarged to 4$\frac{1}{2}$-liters, the torque and power increases being made to match the increasingly heavy coachwork chosen by the clientele. The style of all these cars was as impressive as ever. By 1939 the gearing had also been changed to provide an "overdrive" top gear. This 1939 Sedanca Coupe is typical of the immediate prewar breed.

By the late 1930s, coachwork engineering was advancing. Early cars all used a wooden skeleton, but by the late 1930s, the wood was increasingly reinforced by steel, especially for door pillars and roof surrounds.

the car. The new client was offered a totally new type of Bentley – a new type of automobile, indeed – one that had not previously existed. There was even more performance than before, but this time around the performance came quietly, and in an altogether softer and more feline way. Furthermore, his car could be serviced at one of the celebrated chain of Rolls-Royce dealerships, which now extended across great Britain.

This approach worked well, and the figures proved it. Bentley sales figures, which had struggled to beat 200 cars a year in the final Cricklewood years, immediately leapt to 500 a year, and beyond. If Rolls-Royce could have given more attention to the cars, rather than to the magnificent V-12 aircraft engines, which were rapidly taking over, that figure might have been pushed up even further.

Nevertheless, by the mid-1930s, Rolls-Royce had not only gathered up the wreckage, but had convincingly rebuilt the Bentley marque and its reputation. It was a great start to the "Rolls-Bentley" era, which was set to mature even more convincingly in postwar years.

The new Bentley was very different from the Rolls-Royce Phantom II. It had different cylinder head, carburetion, gearbox ratios, rear axle, and chassis frame, plus a series of unique coach built styles. More than

seen how, and why. By the mid-1930s, the original type of Bentley clientele, who were lovers of the "Big Bloody Thump," the sports cars with a motor racing image, had melted away, and gone off to buy similar cars like the Meadows-engined Invictas and Lagondas, which still retained an atmosphere of cars from the 1920s. Those

buyers would not return – and, in many ways, Rolls-Royce did not miss them.

The new type of client who flocked to the new Bentley – still rich, still able to have his cars driven by a chauffeur if necessary, but also wanting more comfort and more up-to-date styling – was different. But so was

The Rolls-Royce Phantom III of the 1936 – 1939 period was the most complex automobile the company had ever attempted, for it had a brand-new V-12 engine, and coil spring independent suspension. Many cars had big and lofty formal coachwork, but this was an owner-driver "sports saloon."

that, the Bentley was a fast car, capable of more than 90 miles per hour, while a 20/25 struggled to beat 75 miles per hour – and the waiting lists soon built up.

This was the beginning of a golden period for the company, for the Bentley's success more than made up for a slow decline in sales of the Rolls-Royce 20/25 and Phantom II. Body styles continued to change steadily, with younger and more ambitious companies like Park

Ward and Gurney Nutting beginning to use all-metal coachwork instead of the traditional wood-based skeletons, whose origins stretched way back to the eighteenth and nineteenth centuries.

Coachbuilders, though, had an ongoing, and seemingly unstoppable, problem. Every year, it seemed, bodies seemed to get heavier, as more and more equipment was added. Rolls-Royce fought a losing

battle against this trend, and in 1936, all chassis were updated to deal with the problem. By the end of 1936, the Bentley had become a 4^1/4-liter (its engine size being increased to 4,257 cc); the "small" Rolls-Royce had become a 25/30 (also with the 4,257 cc engine, and capable of 80 miles per hour); and there was an exceedingly complex new Phantom III, powered by a brand new 60-degree V-12 engine of 7,340 cc.

There was, at least, one attempt at rationalization, in that the bore and stroke of the V-12 (82.55 x 114.3 mm/$3^1/4$ x $4^1/2$ inches) were the same as those of the

The Rolls-Royce Wraith (not Silver Wraith – that model would follow later) of 1938 was the last, and the most modern, of the prewar models. Still with traditional coach built bodywork and that noble radiator grille style, the Wraith had a $4^1/2$-litre engine, and coil spring independent suspension.

20/25 or Bentley $3^1/2$-liter "Six." Most lovers of larger American cars will realize why Rolls-Royce chose a V-12 engine, rather than a straight-eight, for compared with the old Phantom II "Six" it was a space saver. The wheelbase of a "standard" Phantom III was eight inches shorter than that of the normal "long" Phantom II, yet coachwork offerings were actually larger than before.

Rolls-Royce enthusiasts were originally reluctant to admit that the V-12 engine gave a lot of trouble. It was surely significant that no military use was ever found for the V-12, nor was it revived after World War II. Teething troubles were many and various, especially with the hydraulic tappets, which were new to Rolls-Royce (though familiar to North American carmakers).

In 1938 and 1939, Bentley dabbled with two highly distinctive new styles on the existing 4½-liter chassis. This rather tightly profiled two-door sedan, called the Paulin car after its French stylist, could cruise at well over 100 miles per hour. It even raced at Le Mans, with honor, in postwar years. No serious plans to produce this car, in numbers, were apparently made.

Contemporary lubricants tended to generate sludge, which tended to block up the tappets, and eventually to harm the rotating parts of the engine. This, in part, accounts for the small number of V-12s that have survived to this day.

The Phantom III, though, was the first Rolls-Royce to adopt independent front suspension (years before a Bentley ever had this feature), a conventional-looking coil spring/wishbone layout, in which the coils ran in an oil-filled box, and where there were definite resemblances to the contemporary General Motors layouts. For Rolls-Royce, i.f.s. was not chosen to improve the road-holding, but to provide a softer ride, and in this aim it was certainly successful.

Nor did the V-12 engine give a lot more performance, for complete cars tended to have lofty and heavy formal bodywork, and to weigh in at well over 5,500 pounds. Independent road tests suggested that 92 miles per hour was possible, but no more, and that the fuel consumption could be no more than 8 miles per gallon. However, these cars were not meant to be high performers, but to offer the ultimate in refinement, equipment, style, and image. In Europe, after all, the only credible rival to use a V-12 engine came from Hispano-Suiza, for Daimler's sleeve-valve Double Six types were long gone.

Rolls-Royce then had two more automotive innovations to announce before it got down to serious long-term planning. With sales at Derby tending to stagnate, and with more and more space being needed to produce Merlin aircraft engines, top managers had realized that they must surely rationalize the product range.

But that was for the future. For the present, the Rolls-Royce 25/30 gave way to the new Wraith in 1938, this car having a new 136-inch wheelbase chassis, which was effectively a scaled down Phantom III. Built only in 1938 and 1939, a total of 491 Wraiths were completed before war broke out.

The second innovation, of what was called the "overdrive" gearbox, was only made available in 1939 on the Bentley 4^{1}/4-liter model. Before the introduction of this gearbox, Rolls-Royce had been picking up complaints. New high-speed roads in Europe, particularly in Germany and Italy, meant Bentleys were sometimes being over-revved for long distances on these highways, which did nothing for the life of their engines. Bentley's solution was to realign the gearbox internal ratios, so that third gear became the direct ratio, while fourth became a geared-up "overdrive."

In the meantime, Rolls-Royce had set about a root-and-branch change to the cars they would build in the future. The credit for pushing through the "Rationalized Range" concept goes mainly to two engineers – Ernest Hives and W.A.Robotham.

From 1937 (even before the Wraith and the "overdrive" Bentley had gone on sale), they began to press for a rationalization strategy. Rolls-Royce had become very inward-looking, arrogantly assuming that it always knew best. Only after the manufacturing methods of other companies were studied, was the company convinced otherwise. After all, if Cadillac could share pieces with Buick, why shouldn't Bentley and Rolls-Royce cooperate?

Purely in business terms, productivity and profitability also had to be addressed. Only 1,000 rolling chassis were being built every year at Derby, yet there were three product lines, three chassis frames, two totally different engines, and a myriad of different body styles being grafted to them. Not only was this unwieldy, but the cost of labor was rising sharply.

W.A. Robotham made a series of startling recommendations, one being that the company should develop a single new, yet very versatile, chassis frame, and another being that a new range of in-line engines – of four, six and eight cylinders – should be evolved to

The original Bentley Corniche prototype of 1939, which rode on the still secret Mk V chassis, was styled by Paulin, but bodied by Van Vooren of Paris. In high-speed testing, it had an eventful 6,785-mile career, and was partly disassembled so that the chassis could be repaired at Derby. The body shell remained in France and, as bad luck would have it, was destroyed by a German bomb while on the quayside at Dieppe in 1940. If war had not intervened, this car might have had a production future.

match. He also concluded that the company should finally begin making its own body shells, of a substantially standard design. Buying one of the existing "favored" coachbuilders should do this. Park Ward was the chosen candidate. Accordingly, the

company would, finally, be able to build complete cars.

Although this strategy was approved, the outbreak of World War II caused delays. Even so, the first of the "rationalized" chassis was shown under the stillborn Bentley Mk V of late 1939. But the new engines were

not ready until the mid-1940s. The first complete cars – actually Bentley Mk VI types – would be unveiled after the war, in 1946.

Although the Bentley Mk V never officially went on sale, it was a very important link between the "Derby" type of cars of the 1930s, and the original Mk VI of 1946. Only 19 chassis were laid down, and 11 cars completed.

Compared with the "overdrive" $4^{1}/4$-liter model, which it replaced, the Mk V was a direct evolution – the first to show off the "rationalization" strategy. It was the first product to get the brand new chassis frame, and the first Bentley with independent front suspension. It was to be sold complete with a standardized Park Ward body shell.

The chassis itself, stiffer than ever, with a center cruciform, rode on a 124-inch wheelbase. The independent front suspension, by coil springs and wishbones, was a simpler evolution of the Rolls-Royce Wraith and Phantom III types. Rear suspension, by half-elliptic springs, had the long-established shock absorber stiffness-control feature. As ever, the brakes featured the Hispano-inspired mechanical (friction) servo assistance. At this stage, though, the overhead-valve engine, and the four-speed "overdrive" gearbox were actually improved versions of the outgoing $4^{1}/4$-liter model.

Bentley intended to steer most customers toward the latest Park Ward shell, whose four-door style reflected improvements on the existing $4^{1}/4$-liter styles.

Though postwar styles would be very different, in 1939/1940 there were still vast headlamps standing proud on each side of the radiator, though the running boards under the passenger doors had virtually disappeared.

This was a car that never actually reached the public. They had to wait for the shooting and bombing to end before they could buy a new Bentley. Eleven of the nineteen chassis laid down, were completed in 1939 and 1940, but all of these cars were put to wartime use by Rolls-Royce executives or their suppliers. However, one car did go to G. Geoffrey Smith, editor-in chief of Autocar magazine. The motoring media was also allowed to drive Managing Director Arthur Sidgreaves' car, to keep interest in the new developments alive.

In September 1939, however, all of Rolls-Royce's automotive strategies and plans had to be put on ice, for immediately after the outbreak of war, the company turned its undivided attention to building aircraft engines. Not that the Hives/Robotham rationalization policy was abandoned. In every spare minute – and there were a few, even in the depths of the war – the project went ahead.

Even so, it would be 1946 before the company's postwar plans became clear.

INTERMISSION: AIRCRAFT ENGINES THAT MADE HISTORY

When World War I broke out in 1914, Rolls-Royce began to develop aircraft engines. The first, broadly based on the layout of a Renault V-8, was the Eagle. Introduced in 1915, it produced 225 horsepower, and was eventually boosted to 360 horsepower by 1918. The Rolls-Royce Eagle, Hawk and Falcon were all exceptionally successful in Royal Flying Corps flying machines.

Between the wars, the company developed the enormous 2,300 horsepower supercharged R-Type V-12, which not only powered the Supermarine seaplanes which dominated the Schneider Trophy race, but were later used in successful Land Speed Record and Water Speed Record machinery too.

Even so, it was the 27-litre supercharged V-12 Merlin, really a smaller "productionized" derivative of the R-Type, which became a legend. Designed in the 1930s, and first put into production at Derby for use in the Hawker Hurricane and Supermarine Spitfire fighter aircraft, it also went on to power the four-engined Avro Lancaster bomber, the twin-engined De Havilland Mosquito, the Mustang P51B, and other less glamorous aircraft.

Demand for the Merlin was limitless, which explains why the government helped Rolls-Royce to build a new factory at Crewe, in Staffordshire, England, another close

Once Rolls-Royce's British Merlin engine was mated to the Mustang fighter from the United States, the result was a remarkably fast, effective long-range fighter, the best of the World War II machines.

to Glasgow in Scotland, and why Britain's Ford concern also produced Merlins near Manchester, while Packard of the United States built them for the Mustang and other aircraft. Later, an unsupercharged derivative, the Meteor, was developed to power battle tanks. The British car company, Rover, was the principal manufacturer of this engine.

Early Merlins produced 1,000 horsepower, but by 1944 this output had been doubled, and there was a larger relative of this engine, the 37-liter Griffon, to take over after that. More than 168,000 Merlins were eventually made (55,523 by Packard in the United States). Some insist that this engine won the war. Hyperbole, no doubt, but in the euphoria of victory,

one can see why.

To follow up, Rolls-Royce was also the British pioneer of gas-turbine ("jet") engines. These were originally fitted to the Gloster Meteor fighter, which did so much to counter the V1 "flying bomb" menace. In postwar years Rolls-Royce jets would take an increasing share of the civil and military market, both as propeller turbines or pure thrust units. By the end of the century, Rolls-Royce "Trent" engines were among the most powerful and the most fuel-efficient civil power units in the world.

CHAPTER *Four*

TRADITIONAL MOTORING

IN THE 1940S & 1950S

EVEN DURING WORLD WAR II, when the company's greatest efforts went into producing tens of thousands of magnificent, powerful, and indomitable V-12 aircraft engines, Rolls-Royce/Bentley's staff still found time – made time, even – to think about their automotive future. The work that had already gone into producing the stillborn Mk V was not allowed to go to waste.

aircraft engines. Once the fighting was over, and demand for aircraft engines slumped, it was decided to reequip the company's modern aircraft factory in Crewe, and to use the more up-to-date facilities to reduce production costs.

The factory at Crewe had been commissioned because war was looming at the end of the 1930s. Huge orders were already being placed for the magnificent new Rolls-Royce V-12 aircraft engine, and it was clear that the Derby factory was not big enough, and simply could not cope with the demand.

Helped along by government finance, an entirely new factory was set up at Pyms Lane, Crewe, in Staffordshire, England, a town previously known purely as an important "railway" center. When completed, it was a sizeable complex, which would eventually prove large enough to produce ample Bentley and Rolls-Royce cars for the next fifty years.

The Crewe factory was much larger than the motorcar section of Derby had ever been, so the choice

Even while the fighting continued, and V-12 Merlin engines continued to flood out of the factories, several major automotive decisions were made, one being that the company should completely renew the model program. Three 1939-40 models – the Bentley Mk V, Rolls-Royce Wraith, and Phantom III, all modern cars –

would be discontinued.

Not only that, but the company took a deep breath, and began looking for increased sales – in fact, a considerable increase over the level of the late 1930s was planned. To do this, the directors concluded, car assembly would have to be separated from building was an easy one to make. The factory would be needed for the manufacture of complete automobiles, so more space was needed to deal with the final assembly, painting and trimming body shells, and for assembling those bodies on rolling chassis.

After the last Merlin aircraft engines and their larger derivatives, the Griffons, were manufactured at Crewe in 1945, the facilities were stripped and the buildings reequipped for automobile assembly. The very first Crewe-built cars, announced in 1946, were the Rolls-Royce Silver Wraith, and the original "standard steel" Bentley Mk VI, whose body shells were provided by the Pressed Steel Co. Ltd. of Cowley, near Oxford. At this time, the days of alternative wheelbases on "standard" cars were banished to the nostalgia cupboard. For Bentley and Rolls-Royce sedans and sporting cars (but not, of course, for limousines), all bodies would have to be built on the same basis.

Not that this meant the end of the luscious, individually styled, craftsman-built body shells. On one hand, the original postwar Rolls-Royces – to be launched in 1946, and christened "Silver Wraith" –

For postwar usage, Rolls-Royce commissioned its first "standard steel" body shell. Manufactured by the Pressed Steel Co. Limited, this was first seen on the Bentley Mk VI of 1946 and, in slightly modified form, would be used until 1955.

Left: Viewed from the side, the Bentley Mk VI was simple, graceful and elegant. The style was clearly an evolution of the shapes of the late 1930s. In 1949, this model would be joined by the Rolls-Royce Silver Dawn, which looked almost identical.

Below: Comfort, but not a great deal of leg room, in the rear seat of the Bentley Mk VI. All that wood, leather, and folding picnic tables, plus the passenger vanity mirrors, came as standard equipment.

Above: This was the fascia/instrument panel of the Bentley Mk VI. On this right-hand drive car, note that the gear shift is on the right of the driver's seat, close to the door panel.

would all have special coachwork, while the company would still make its latest chassis available to the same coachbuilders. In the medium term, there were hopes of introducing a special line of fast, sporting cars to follow up the Corniche/"Embiricos" experiments of 1938 and 1939.

Although Britain's postwar coach building industry was a mere shadow of its former self, there were still some high-price/high-standard concerns that looked forward to serving Rolls-Royce and Bentley. For the time being, the future of the industry seemed to be assured. After the war, Park Ward, H.J. Mulliner, Hooper, and Freestone & Webb were still vibrant, though Thrupp & Maberly, Vanden Plas, and Gurney Nutting had either disappeared, or had been absorbed into larger corporations. Park Ward, which Rolls-Royce had bought in the late 1930s, was effectively an "in-house" specialist, and would be joined by H.J. Mulliner before the end of the 1950s.

For the next twenty years, Rolls-Royce would follow the same pragmatic path. First, they established the philosophy of building standard-looking Bentleys and Rolls-Royces, while looking for ways to offer specialized versions to flesh out the range. It was a very measured way of doing business, in which continuity and profit were paramount. In twenty years – from 1945 to 1965 – there would be only two different chassis generations and two engines.

It took time to clear aircraft engine production facilities out of Crewe, and to finalize arrangements with the Pressed Steel Co. to supply complete body shells. The process of producing cars – more cars than ever before, but still to be made at a steady pace – began in 1946. Rolls-Royce announced its Silver Wraith chassis, on a 127-inch wheelbase in April; one month later Bentley announced the new Mark VI sedan on a shortened version, this time with a 120-inch wheelbase.

Until 1949 the Mark VI would dominate the scene at Crewe, for Rolls-Royce Silver Wraith assembly was at a much slower rate. Then, in 1949, the Rolls-Royce version of the Mark VI – the Silver Dawn – appeared, and redressed the balance. Even so, the only body shells seen at Crewe were of the "standard steel" variety from Pressed Steel. All other shells were constructed by outside specialists.

The Bentley Mk VI was a lineal successor to the "Derby Bentley" types of the 1930s, and was closely related to the new Rolls-Royce Silver Wraith. In a few years, however, an even larger car would be in the range, the positively gargantuan Rolls-Royce Phantom IV, whose wheelbase was even longer, and which had a straight-eight engine.

The new postwar car evolved around an evolutionary version of the 1939-40 Mk V chassis, much updated in detail, and with a direct-drive gearbox instead of the "overdrive" feature. Except for the shorter wheelbase, this looked the same as before, complete with coil spring independent front suspension, and sturdy cruciform crossbracing under the passenger floor. As before, there was centralized chassis lubrication, with a maze of pipes sending oil to the suspension joints.

Although the engine size – 4,257 cc – looked familiar (some basic dimensions from the prewar power unit were still there), this was the first of a new range of standardized engines. Coded B40, B60, and B80, these were closely related four-cylinder, six-cylinder, and eight-cylinder types, all with a new type of light alloy cylinder head that featured overhead intake valves and side exhaust valves.

Though there was no call for a B40-engined private car, it would find extensive light military use, while the B80 would find a home in the Rolls-Royce Phantom IV of 1950, and in many military vehicles. In 1946, however, the automotive operation saw the six-cylinder

As part of its postwar technical strategy, Rolls-Royce developed a closely related family of new engines – four-cylinder (right), six-cylinder (center) and eight-cylinder. The "six" would be used in Bentley and Rolls-Royce private cars after 1945, the "eight" only in the very rare Phantom IV.

B60 as key to its strategic future. As ever, peak power outputs were not revealed, but years later a learned paper read to the Institute of Mechanical Engineering stated that it was 132 horsepower. "It's only a statistic," top engineer Harry Grylls once said, "and who's interested in them?" It was enough to give the Mk VI a 100-mile per hour top speed.

For Rolls-Royce, the real novelty was that this was the very first Bentley/Rolls-Royce product to be assembled in its entirety at the parent factory. The Mk VI, though, was also offered as a rolling chassis, so customers could make their own deal with an

Beginning in 1949, Rolls-Royce produced the Silver Dawn, which shared its basic body shell, and mechanical layout with the contemporary Bentley Mk VI. Originally, the Silver Dawn was only sold on export markets, particularly in North America.

individual coachbuilder. Although there was a brisk demand, the balance swung permanently, to the "standard steel" cars. Of all the Bentleys (Mk VI and R-Type) built on this chassis, 7,521 (or 83 per cent) used the standard style, while 1,302 had special coachwork.

Although the fresh new style was practical and elegant, its lines leaned heavily on the packaging of late-1930s and Mark V Park Ward styles. The long hood, the compact five-seater cabin, and the short tail all looked familiar, though the semirecessed headlamps were new. Interior equipment, seating, the right-hand gear shift, and the fascia layout were all a modern interpretation of several late-1930s themes. The only problem was that the right-side gear shift could not be flipped over for left-hand-drive cars, as the gearbox design precluded that. In 1949, a steering column gear shift became available and this was used instead.

No sooner had the Mk VI gone on sale, than sales

Because the Bentley Mk VI had a separate chassis frame, coachbuilders could still produce special editions. This was a very smart three-door "woody" station wagon, which came from Harold Radford.

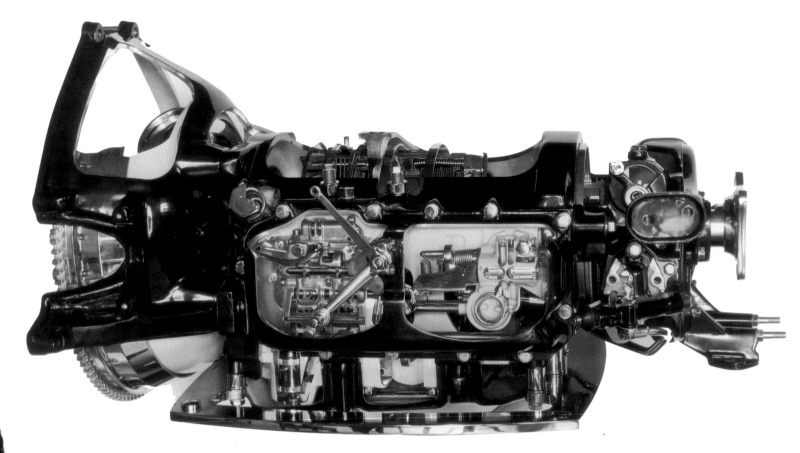

Right: This display model of the RR/GM Hydramatic automatic transmission shows just how complex it was. Not to be rebuilt by the amateur . . .

Below: From late 1952, automatic transmission finally became available – this being an adaptation of the GM Hydra-matic four-speed installation.

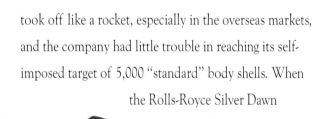

took off like a rocket, especially in the overseas markets, and the company had little trouble in reaching its self-imposed target of 5,000 "standard" body shells. When the Rolls-Royce Silver Dawn appeared in 1949, initially for export only, it complemented, rather than detracted from, the attraction of the Mark VI.

In the meantime, as the only contemporary model to bear the Rolls-Royce radiator, the Silver Wraith carried on flying the flag – and would do so until 1959. Chassis built in the late 1950s had evolved in detail from those produced in 1946, but the basic layout was never changed. In the beginning, the cars ran on a 127-inch wheelbase, with 4,257cc, but from mid-1951 the wheelbase went up to 133 inches, along with an engine stretch to 4,566 cc. This allowed already capacious bodies to become even larger than before.

Automatic transmission arrived in late 1952, optional

at first, but manual transmission soon disappeared from the lists. The 4,887 cc engine took over in 1956. In the meantime, body styles changed slowly, steadily, and sometimes almost imperceptibly from season to season. It needed a real Silver Wraith expert to stand back from a car and say just when it had been built.

Above: The straight-eight cylinder engine used in the Phantom IV models was developed from engines normally fitted to British military vehicles. Effectively, it was the normal Rolls-Royce "six" with an extra two cylinders.

Left: In the early 1950s, Rolls-Royce built the Phantom IV, a longer-wheelbase derivative of the Silver Wraith, and fitted with a straight-eight engine. Available only to royalty and heads of state, 18 such cars were delivered. Customers included Queen Elizabeth II, Princess Margaret, and the Spanish dictator, General Franco. This car was an H.J. Mulliner-bodied DHC.

Although some critics suggested that the Silver Dawn was no more than a "badge-engineered" Mk VI, the clientele didn't seem to mind. Although the chassis, the basic body style, and the basic running gear were just the same, the Rolls-Royce radiator was up front, the fascia layout was different, and the company pushed it hard in some of its traditional export markets. Silver Dawns, in fact, would not be available in the UK until 1953. Beginning in 1949, in fact, Silver Dawns and Mk VIs were assembled on the same assembly line at Crewe.

Five years into its career and only one year before these model were replaced by the evolutionary R-Type body style, the Mark VI/Silver Dawn types inherited the enlarged 4,566 cc engine intended for the still-secret Continental coupe.

This was just one more improvement along the way to modernizing the Rolls-Royce and Bentley range. The R-Type of late 1952 was the one-and-only facelift made to this shell, and it arrived in the autumn of 1952. The "R-Type" (though the Silver Dawn was never renamed), kept the pot boiling very well from 1952 to 1955.

Except for the arrival of an automatic transmission option, there were few changes to the running gear, though twin SU carburetors became standard, even in the United States, where the Mk VI had previously used

a single Stromberg unit. The major change was to the Pressed Steel "standard steel" sedan body style, in which the entire rear end had been reshaped, lengthening the shell by 7.5 inches. In some ways, it perfectly bridged the visual gap between the Mk VI, and the S-Type, which was to follow.

Announced in September 1952, these cars were warmly welcomed, especially as there was now to be an optional automatic transmission. By 1952, automatic gearboxes already figured in most North American line-ups, but no other British marque was so equipped. The Rolls-Royce option came from General Motors in the United States, which provided the Hydra-matic assembly, which had a four-speed transmission and a simple fluid coupling. The traditional Bentley/Rolls-Royce friction-type brake servo was grafted on to the tail of the casing, and gear selection was by a lever and quadrant mounted on the steering column. Optional at first, it was soon fitted to almost every Bentley and Rolls-Royce to be built.

In the meantime, both "standard" cars from Crewe had been overshadowed by a magnificent irrelevance, a monstrously heavy, bulky, and mainly craftsman-built machine. Starting in 1950, and built strictly for "royalty and heads of state," the company built just eighteen Phantom IVs before 1956. Larger, longer, and heavier

than the Silver Wraith – the wheelbase was no less than 145 inches – these cars were powered by the B80 straight-eight engine.

Of the eighteen cars, five went to members of the British Royal Family (Princess, later Queen, Elizabeth, took the first); three went to the ruler of Kuwait; three to the Spanish dictator, General Franco; and Rolls-Royce kept one, which it bodied as a high-performance delivery wagon/endurance car. Companies such as H.J. Mulliner and Hooper bodied most of these machines as sedans, limousines, or landaulettes (with the drivers seat uncovered).

In these days of cheap fuel (especially if one happened to be the ruler of Kuwait), a fuel consumption of less than 8 miles per gallon didn't seem too much of a problem.

In the meantime, Bentley had also gone off on a flight of fantasy, to produce the fast, beautiful, and exclusive R-Type Continental. Though its engineering was based on the R-Type, the basic idea had evolved from that of the late-1930s prototypes – the "Embiricos" coupe, and the original Corniche high-speed sedan. The engineers' intention, simply, was to produce a seriously fast Bentley, one that its customers could enjoy driving far and fast, particularly on the high-speed motor roads of Europe.

Left: H.J. Mulliner & Co. Ltd produced the sleek two-door fastback coupe style of the Bentley R-Type Continental. Although definitely shaped like a coupe, it was still a full four-seater model.

Below: Launched in 1952, the magnificent Bentley Continental R-Type was not only the fastest, but the most expensive Bentley built up to that time. Its top speed was 115 miles per hour.

The running gear was based closely on the forthcoming R-Type evolution of the chassis. The body style could be all new, a smoothly detailed two-door four-seater, really a sedan rather than a coupe; the contract to build the bodies was placed with H.J. Mulliner of London.

The style was a masterpiece, with a proud sedan-style Bentley nose, a roofline lower by 1.5 inches, and a long, smoothly detailed, sloping tail. By 1950s standards, there wasn't a line or a proportion out of place. H.J. Mulliner's weight-saving techniques had produced a body that was 360 pounds lighter than the sedan. It contained as much light alloy as possible, along with aircraft industry attention to many other fixings.

Mechanically, the R-Type Continental's chassis was very close to that of the sedan. The engine itself was a lightly modified 4,566 cc unit at first, and the rear axle ratio was raised considerably. On the R-Type sedan, the ratio was 3.727:1, but for the longer-striding Continental it was raised by no less than 21 per cent, to 3.077:1. Although right-hand drive cars retained their right-hand gear shift, Bentley made another attempt to

provide a satisfactory gear shift for left-hand drive customers. A steering column shift was still available, along with a new center-floor gear shift. Hydra-matic transmission was not available until April 1954.

Here was a car that broke the mold of postwar Bentleys for it could reach 115 miles per hour. No wonder that Britain's "establishment" motoring magazine, *Autocar*, praised its road test car like this:

"This Bentley is a modern magic carpet which annihilates great distances and delivers the occupants well-nigh as fresh as when they started. It is a car Britain may well be proud of, and it is sure to add new luster to the name it bears."

Forget the fact that it was very expensive – in 1953 it cost 58 per cent more than the sedan. In those days, it was not merely a car, but an icon of the British motor industry.

In May 1954, incidentally, there was a major change to the specification, when it was decided to standardize a larger 4,887 cc, version of the engine. On reflection, this was an ideal way of proving the power unit, which was destined to go into every original S-type. No fewer than 82 of the 208 R-Type Continentals got this engine.

In the meantime, the Bentley R-Type/Rolls-Royce Silver Dawn, both direct descendants of the Mk VI,

reached full maturity early in 1955, when the last cars were assembled at Crewe, but now it was time for the big change. In came the Rolls-Royce Silver Cloud/Bentley S-Type family, for which the well-known engine/transmission would continue, but almost every other component was new. In April 1955, it was all-change time at Crewe.

Up until then in the postyears, Bentleys had always outsold Rolls-Royces, but that was about to change. From that moment, Rolls-Royce and Bentley specifications became very close indeed (except in their radiator styling and – for a time at least – their state of engine tune). From 1959, and the arrival of the new V-8 engine, there were no mechanical differences of any type.

Both models shared a new 123-inch wheelbase chassis, both using closely similar versions of the latest Pressed Steel "standard steel" body. UK prices, too, were similar – in 1955 a Bentley S cost $13,073, while a Rolls-Royce Silver Cloud I cost $13,428. For the moment, though, it was Bentley's sporting heritage that continued to give it an edge. Soon, however, Rolls-Royce would begin to outsell Bentley, and would hold that advantage until the 1980s.

Although many rivals were turning to unit-body structures, Rolls-Royce was not ready to go down that route. Accordingly, the Silver Cloud/S-Type kept a separate chassis, a standard-style body shell, beam axle rear suspension, and a final development of the famous six-cylinder engine.

Because the standard-style Rolls-Royce was now freely available at home, the "Spirit of Ecstasy" mascot gradually began to outrank the "Flying B," as most of the marketing effort went behind the Rolls-Royce version. Although the Bentley S1 outsold the Silver Cloud by three to two, later Bentleys would be outpaced.

Although critics suggested that the interior packaging was poor (massive seats and a floor that was

Below: Forty years later, Rolls-Royce claimed that the style of the 1955 Silver Cloud inspired the birth of the late-1990s Silver Seraph, and issued this artist's rendering to make their point.

Right: Most Silver Clouds, or their Bentley S-series sister cars, were supplied with two-tone colour schemes. Sometimes the darker shade was applied to the roof or . . .

relatively so high off the ground didn't help), the new shape was a gracious masterpiece. When the new Silver Seraph/Arnage types came along in late 1990s, these cars were often quoted as ideals to be replicated. Compared with the Silver Dawn/R-Type, though, this was a bigger car in all respects – with a 123-inch wheelbase and 1.5-inch wider wheel tracks, and the

Sometimes the lighter shade of two-tone color schemes was painted on the roof. It seemed to work well in all cases. The JB1000 registration number indicates that this car was a "Jack Barclay" (Bentley dealership) demonstrator.

engine enlarged to 4,887 cc, no wonder the unladen weight was up, to 4,480 pounds.

Here was a car in which there was little technical innovation. The steering was initially low geared, but within a year, power-assisted steering had arrived. The engine got a new-type aluminum cylinder head, though, as ever, Rolls-Royce/Bentley never said what peak outputs actually were. We may guess at about 155 horsepower at first, and up to 178 horsepower before the power unit was dropped four years later.

Because this was a car with a near silent engine and automatic transmission, the actual driving seemed to take care of itself. It was the fixtures and fittings that made such an impact. Deep pile carpets; thick walnut panels on the fascia, the door tops, and the picnic tables in the rear compartment; enormously plushy seats; and a complex new heating/ventilation system all made an impression.

With a 105 miles per hour top speed, it was a brisk, mobile drawing room, which improved gradually over four years. A 4-inch longer-wheelbase version was

The Silver Cloud was a large and lofty car, as this nicely posed shot, with its charming lady driver, makes clear. The backdrop, incidentally, is London's Albert Memorial.

available from late 1957; optional air conditioning appeared in 1956; and the engines became more powerful in late 1957. As ever, special coachwork could be fitted if the client insisted, and if he took his chassis to an approved coachbuilder. This, though, was only a beginning – for a V-8 engine was on the way.

It was 1959, fourteen years after the end of the war,

before Bentley/Rolls-Royce announced its first new engine in two decades – an all-new V-8, with alloy cylinder block and head castings. Yet the cars were not restyled to suit – squeezing the new V-8 into existing engine bays had been a major problem.

Rolls-Royce looked hard at Cadillac and Chrysler products before finalizing their own engine. After facing

up to the ongoing "horsepower race" among Detroit's carmakers, they started making new V-8s in 1959. It was, in every way, a clean break from old to new, there being no carryover components or facilities.

Although the new V-8 was larger than the old straight six – much wider, of course, though about the same length, and already a 6½-liter unit – it was

actually 30 pounds lighter. Don't christen it a lightweight, though – in unit with the Hydra-matic automatic transmission, it turned the scales at 890 pounds.

As usual, there were no official peak power figures, though 200 horsepower, along with 325 ft-lbs of torque was a good guess. On road test, the top speed had risen from 105 miles per hour to 113 miles per hour. Other technical improvements included power assisted steering as standard, while central chassis lubrication had been abandoned. In place were individual grease points, each with its own reservoir, needing attention at 10,000 miles (or one year, if a car was driven little).

Management, however, treated this only as an interim car, which explains why it had only a three-year life. The Silver Cloud III/S3 of 1962 – 1965 that followed was an important model for several reasons. It was the last car from Crewe to have a separate chassis frame, and the first to have four (twinned) headlamps. It also signaled the point at which Bentley sales began to slip back into the shadows.

After seven years of steadily rising sales, Rolls-

To replace the long-running Silver Wraith, Rolls-Royce introduced the Phantom V limousine in 1959, complete with its 6,230 cc V-8 engine, and a seven-seater limousine cabin. There were several styles; this mid-1960s example is by James Young.

Royce management spent more money with Pressed, in reshaping the front end of the body shell: this involved lowering the radiator shells, and positioning the four headlamps, in pairs, at each side of the new grille.

Under the skin, there were more detail improvements, with reduced power-steering efforts, and more power (perhaps 15 – 20 horsepower) to the still-modern engine.

In the meantime, Rolls-Royce had finally replaced the long-running Silver Wraith with an even larger, even more dignified, and even more magisterial machine known as the Phantom V. Although production eventually

By the end of the 1970s, the British royal household had a fleet of five Rolls-Royce Phantoms in the Royal Mews. Clockwise from the front are a Phantom IV, another Phantom IV, a high-roof Phantom V, a high-roof Phantom VI, and another high-roof Phantom V.

Two versions of the Bentley S1 Continental – a drop-head coupe and a fixed-head coupe, both bodied by Park Ward, pose in front of a BOAC Argonaut of the 1950s.

H.J. Mulliner's Bentley Continental S-Series style changed only in detail between 1955 and the mid-1960s, when this particular S3 was constructed. Bentley always called them saloons, though most enthusiasts call them coupes.

fell away to a trickle of special orders, this model (and its lightly-modified successor, the Phantom VI), would remain in production until 1990, by which time just 889 cars – 516 of them Phantom Vs – had been made.

Based very closely on the engineering of the new Silver Cloud II, the Phantom V ran on a 145-inch wheelbase version of that car's chassis, with the same V-8 engine, automatic transmission, suspensions, power-assisted steering, and drum brake system. The Phantom V would become the Phantom VI in 1968, with no important style changes, but with detail specification changes, including the use of separate air conditioning

In the mid-1950s, Park Ward and H.J. Mulliner drop-head coupe styles on the Bentley S1 Continental were remarkably similar. This car, in fact, is using a Park Ward body shell. Inset: In late 1959, Rolls-Royce issued this simple "ghosted" drawing of the new Silver Cloud II/Bentley S2 models, showing that the bulky new V-8 engine completely filled the underhood space.

installations for front and rear compartments. Then years after that, in 1978, the Phantom VI would finally get the larger (6,750 cc) V-8 engine, with the three-speed GM400 automatic transmission, but to the very end these cars were always produced with drum brakes.

Bodies, though, were invariably seven-seater limousines or (very rarely) state landaulettes, from H.J. Mulliner or Park Ward. In the beginning, there were a few sedans from James Young. Although all these cars were very bulky, their overall proportions, and in particular their noses, looked much like those of the Silver Clouds; incidentally, there never was a Bentley version of these cars.

H.J. Mulliner was taken over by Rolls-Royce in 1959

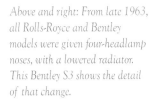

Above and right: From late 1963, all Rolls-Royce and Bentley models were given four-headlamp noses, with a lowered radiator. This Bentley S3 shows the detail of that change.

Compared with the earlier type, the Bentley S3 had a more powerful 6,230 cc engine (its compression ratio was raised to 9.0:1), a lowered radiator shell, and restyled front wings to suit.

and merged with Park Ward in 1962, after which Rolls-Royce eventually settled on a standard Mulliner style for these magnificent limousines. Although there was a small amount of tooling at the coach-building works in northwest London, every one of these cars was made to order. Body construction, trimming and fitting out took many months to complete. Some of the body shell, incidentally, had aluminum paneling, which helped stave off corrosion in later years.

The basic specification, which included air conditioning, fold-up occasional seats in the spacious rear compartment, and separate radio installation in front and rear, was only a start to negotiations, for a long list of optional extras was also available. The vast majority of sales would be to large corporations, local authorities, and even up-market "weddings-and-funerals" concerns, who all needed to take a "brave pill" before reading the invoice for the finished job.

Because there was so much handwork in these magnificent machines, there was no question of assembly line manufacture, and no way chassis and body shells could be shared with other models. There was, perhaps, very little profit in the program. Rolls-Royce, however, knew that it needed such a presence at the very top of the market; if it withdrew, companies

like Mercedes-Benz would step in very quickly.

Queen Elizabeth eventually took delivery of three very special Phantoms – two Vs and a VI – all of which shared the same ultra-high-roof body style, with extra glass area These cars also had a very large glass rear window, which could be covered over with shaped aluminum panels. In the 1980s the queen also took delivery of a fourth standard (Mulliner) style Phantom VI. None were ever given registration numbers, and all these cars would provide dignified and reliable service well into the new century.

Such cars, of course, had an entirely different character from the Bentley S-Type Continentals that were produced from 1955 to 1966, for those were extremely elegant machines. These cars – S1, S2, and S3 were sold in a wonderful variety of body styles.

Like previous Continentals, the S-Type ran on a lightly modified sedan-style chassis, clothed in sleeker bodywork. Continentals tracked the sedan's major changes – S2 in late 1959 (with V-8 engines), and S3s in late 1962 (with more power and four-headlamp noses).

The Park Ward-bodied Bentley Continental became the S3 in 1963, complete with the "oriental" four-headlamp nose style, but with no other sheet metal changes.

Eventually a great variety of styles were offered – not only two-door or four-door, coupe or sedan, but convertibles too – from H.J. Mulliner-Park-Ward, (Mulliner-Park-Ward after the merger) and James Young.

Because Continentals used more aluminum in their body construction, they were usually lighter – sometimes more than 400 pounds – and their acceleration figures were always more impressive. For these coachbuilders, Bentley provided the chassis complete with a radiator, firewall, and floor-pan. The sedan-type radiator grille (lowered slightly) was retained, and when the factory switched from two to four headlamps in 1962/1963, Continental styles obediently followed suit.

The original S-Type Continentals were announced in the autumn of 1955, when there were three "official" coupe styles, from H.J. Mulliner (coupe), and Park Ward (convertible and closed coupe). Before long James Young also joined in.

Then, in late 1957, came a real breakthrough. Using the same Continental chassis, H.J. Mulliner produced a four-door sedan style, and called it the "Flying Spur."

Officially this was not a Continental at first, though eventually Mulliner persuaded the company that it should be. In fact, the entire front end of the Flying Spur was the same as that of the HJM Continental. James Young and Hooper soon followed suit with their own four-door cars.

The next big upheaval came in the autumn of 1959, when Park Ward introduced a brand-new V-8-engined two-door body style, with a striking theme and a distinctive "straight-through" fender line linking headlamps to tail lamps. This would be Park Ward's standard offering for six years, introducing styling that would eventually appear in the standard sedan form.

S-Type Continental sales were always encouraging and steady. A total of 1,131 of all versions would be built, at a rate of about 110 a year, but there were no new styles after 1959. Even so, and just to confuse things a little, a few "Continental" bodies were produced with Rolls-Royce radiators and identities.

All this, however, was drawing to a close, for the last few separate-chassis Bentleys were produced at Crewe in the autumn of 1965, and the last Continental was shipped to an overseas customer in January 1966. From that moment, an entirely different type of Rolls-Royce/Bentley would take over.

CHAPTER Five

SILVER SHADOW & T-SERIES

NEW CARS, NEW STYLES, NEW ENGINEERING

THE BIGGEST EVER TECHNICAL CHANGE IN THE COMPANY'S HISTORY CAME IN 1965. Ten years of deep thinking, of design and redesign, and development had gone into it. The result was a new style, a new name, and an entirely fresh way of building cars. Except for their V-8 engine and transmission, the new Rolls-Royce Silver Shadow and Bentley T-Series, twins in all but badging, were totally different from the last of the separate-chassis cars they replaced.

This was not ahead of its time, for a complete design revolution had been overdue at Crewe for some years. Top management knew it, the sales staff knew it, as did the design and engineering staffs, but financial and marketing caution had ensured continuous delays. In the end it was competition – competition from the rivals – in the late 1950s, and into the 1960s, which saw them beginning to adopt new body styles and technical innovation, which put them ahead of Bentley and Rolls-Royce.

It wasn't that the staff at Crewe was moribund, but that their new cars, by tradition, had always taken a long time to mature. The company's distinguished chairman, Lord Hives, once commented, "research is development, but done slowly."

By the late 1950s, though, there was no holding back. Having watched the marketplace very carefully, the company finally decided to make a clean break with its traditions, and to move into a new future. Not merely a step, but a real leap, for there was much time to be made up.

Almost all of the company's well-honed traditions – separate chassis frames, drum brakes, beam rear axles, and traditional styling – would all have to be cast away, and not gradually over time, but together. This was

certain to cost more than any previous Rolls-Royce project and it was once again confirmed that there was not time, finance, or scope for Bentley and Rolls-Royce versions to be technically different. Essentially they would have to be the same.

In earlier years there had been a lot of ill-informed

media criticism about the company's "old-fashioned cars," so it was almost as if the management team's patience had finally snapped. If change and innovation was being demanded, then they could certainly expect to see a lot of that.

By the early 1960s, the new V-8 engine had arrived.

Left: Except for its engine and gearbox, the Silver
Shadow/Bentley T-Series cars were totally new. This was the first
type of car from Crewe to have a unit construction body shell, self-
leveling all-independent suspension, and four-wheel disc brakes.

Above: This is the anatomy of the Silver Shadow laid bare in an
"exploded" drawing showing all the technical features. Even in its
original state, this was by far the most complex car ever to be launched
by Rolls-Royce. Incidentally, the floor pan was welded to the
superstructure during assembly, producing a rigid monocoque structure.

For Rolls-Royce, the V-8 engine, seen here in Silver Shadow tune, was a complex piece of equipment, though the company had clearly looked at the best of North American engineering when developing it. The cylinder block and cylinder heads were all cast from aluminum alloy.

Now it was time to introduce a unit-construction body shell, all-independent suspension, four-wheel-disc brakes, self-leveling controls, and high-pressure hydraulics, plus a new type of automatic transmission. Perhaps that would be enough?

Prototypes of a new project along those lines, coded "Tibet" within the factory, started road testing in 1958. This was thought to be too large, and was soon displaced by the "Burma" design, which was a lower, narrower and altogether smaller car. In 1960 the company was convinced that "Burma" was what it needed in the future, even though the capital cost of the development would be substantial. The bare bones of that four-door sedan car, and its very squared-up three-box styling, were painstakingly developed, and then put on sale in 1965. It would continue to sell until 1980. Under the skin, the platform and running gear would then be the basis for yet another generation of Rolls-Royce and Bentley cars, and would not go out of use until the end of the century.

The style of the Bentley T-Series (seen here) and its sister car, the Rolls-Royce Silver Shadow, was simple but nicely detailed. Because it was based on a unit-construction (monocoque) structure, however, it was no longer economically practical for specialists to produce different styles.

This was the era in which Bentley, which in terms of numbers built had been a dominant partner from the mid-1930s, gradually seemed to slip back into the shadows in favor of Rolls-Royce – which was, after all, the parent company and the senior brand. From about 1960, it was clear that top management had decided to reemphasize the Rolls-Royce brand. Starting with the V-8 engined Silver Cloud II, the Rolls-Royce emphasis was gradually, but persistently, made clear. From the launch of this important new range of cars in the mid-1960s, it would become the dominant theme.

It was the biggest change in the history of the company. Apart from the V-8 engine itself, and even here there were important changes, almost every component was new, or drastically altered. Though management had insisted on keeping a cap on costs, this was as near as possible to a "ground-up" project. The design and engineering team had seen it as a fantastic

opportunity, while the sales and marketing staff saw it as an enormous challenge.

Not only was this the very first Crewe product to have a unit construction, but it was also graced by a rather severe four-door body style, which looked smaller than it actually was. The two cars were almost identical. As far as body shells were concerned, the only difference was to the individual hood pressings, which had to match the radiator shells.

Although tooling and manufacture of a monocoque was expensive, Rolls-Royce hoped it would remain on sale for at least ten years. As it turned out, the four-door shell was listed for fifteen years, and the platform survived into the new century.

The new car was several inches lower than before, and there were packaging improvements to the cabin. The new car ran on a 3.5-inch shorter wheelbase, and was 8.5 inches shorter than the old Silver Cloud. Even so, it was still heavy, at 4,650 pounds. This was the first Rolls-Royce/Bentley sedan styled with one long, smooth, slightly curving line between the front corners and the tail lamp shrouds. This was not a shape that

The Crewe factory in the mid-1960s, just before the Silver Shadow was ready to be launched. The stark, utilitarian, 1940s architecture is obvious.

Because the new Silver Shadow had a monocoque structure, it was almost impossible for independent coachbuilders to produce specialist styles on that base. James Young of Bromley tried its best in 1965 - 1966, but could only make a two-door version of the four-door sedan. It was difficult to distinguish the types, and only 50 were ever sold. James Young closed down after that task was completed. Inset: The independent front suspension of the original Silver Shadow/T-Series was a simple double wishbone layout, but with no bush compliance to minimize road noise. That would follow in the 1970s.

Deliveries of the new four-door Silver Shadow began in 1966. This was one of the very first examples.

Left: By spending a fortune on new tooling, Rolls-Royce's subsidiary, Mulliner-Park-Ward, succeeded in developing a shapely two-door version of the Silver Shadow saloon. Announced in 1966, this used the same complex, high-tech. floor pan, but had an entirely new superstructure. Both Rolls-Royce and Bentley versions were available, this being the Bentley .....

....and this being the Rolls-Royce. Mechanically the two cars were identical(right).

out that too-direct steering would affect the handling if there were unplanned movements. But it was in vain. In the future, much work went into improving the road holding and response of this complex chassis.

This was the first-ever Rolls-Royce to have disc brakes, which were controlled by complex layout of pipes and controls. Three different circuits operated at very high hydraulic pressure. A pump ran off the engine, with reserve accumulators for back up. There was no need for servo assistance.

This was much more of an "owner-driver's" car, rather than one that would be chauffeur-driven. Pile carpets, wood, leather and delicately developed controls were all of the usual high standard. Front seats, as ever, were separate, more armchair than racing type; the floor was virtually flat; and the automatic transmission selector lever was on the steering column. Amazingly, air conditioning was still optional – it did not become standard equipment until 1969.

would be easy to face lift – and in fact no attempt to do so was made.

Much technical novelty was hidden away. Suitably updated (spark plugs were now accessible from above) the alloy V-8 engine was up front, now backed by one of two types of automatic transmission. Until 1968, cars for the home market used the old type Hydra-matic, but export versions (and from 1968, all versions) used the modern three-speed GM400 automatic.

Independent suspension was fitted at front and rear.

Wishbones at the front end, and semitrailing arms at the rear, were controlled by coil springs and telescopic dampers. These units were also fitted with hydraulically operated self-leveling rams. Those at the front would eventually be eliminated. As with late-model Silver Clouds, low-geared power-assisted steering was standard.

Originally, the ride was very soft, and the steering felt vague, so there was criticism – not only from the specialist press, but also from the clientele. Management talked persuasively about "the sneeze factor," pointing

In the next few years, the company paid so much attention to the new two-door cars, and to the longer wheelbase derivative of the sedan, that few important changes were made to the four-door sedan. The "I told you so" know-it-alls were pleased to see stiffer suspension and more direct steering arrive in 1968. The modern GM400 transmission was standardized on home market cars soon afterwards. An optional longer wheelbase Silver Shadow (it looked near identical to the ordinary sedan) arrived in 1969.

Next were improvements to keep the car abreast of new American legislation. A new fascia, with much padding and different controls, arrived in 1969, and in 1970 the enlarged, more torquey, $6^1/2$-liter V-8 engine was specified. Until 1977, other changes were mostly in detail – a compliant front suspension package in mid-1972, vast shock-absorbing bumpers (more new American legislation) in late 1973, and yet another redeveloped suspension system, with even fatter tires and a wider rear track, in mid-1974.

Then came the Silver Shadow II/Bentley T2 of 1977, with few visual changes except the fitment of a spoiler under the front bumper, but a nicely integrated package of improvements. The modern fascia/instrument panel layout of the Camargue was adopted, fitted (in part) to make space for the very latest split-level air-conditioning system. Under the skin, immediately

The drop-head coupe derivative of the two-door Silver Shadow was introduced in 1967, and would have an extremely long life. Renamed Corniche in 1971, such cars would be produced until the 1990s.

obvious to anyone who drove the latest cars, was power-assisted rack-and-pinion steering. Here, at last, was a steering layout, that was inch-accurate and felt right.

The end of this model range's life, though, was finally in sight. A new model, coded SZ (it would be badged as a Silver Spirit), was already under development. Though it would keep the same basic floor-pan as before, its shell and detail style, would be very different. In 1980, after 15 years, it was time for the Silver Shadow/T2 cars to give way.

In the meantime, Rolls-Royce had spent ages crafting replacements for the long-running Bentley Continentals. One consequence of electing to use unit construction instead of a sturdy, separate steel chassis was immediately clear. It meant that the days of the under-capitalized independent coachbuilders who relied on craftsmanship and tradition rather than costly tooling, were numbered. Building body shells, often based on wooden framing (but increasingly in the 1950s and 1960s with a metal skeleton), had become a very highly developed craft, which had matured steadily since the first motorcars had been sold in Britain in the 1890s. Such bodies, however, could only take shape on a solid base – a separate and sturdy steel chassis frame.

Accordingly, when Rolls-Royce proposed to build

The first all-steel two-door Rolls-Royce Silver Shadow drop-head coupe appeared in the fall of 1967

all its cars on a steel-based monocoque structure – a combined body/chassis unit – it was simply not going to be possible to supply separate platforms/floorpans ("chassis" in the old-fashioned sense) as these would not be rigid enough to support separate body shells. The whole point of a unit construction body was that

the superstructure (upper body panels, screen and door pillars, roof and body inner structures) all had a part to play in adding rigidity.

Difficult to understand? Think of an eggshell, which is surprisingly strong when intact – but take a slice out of it, and it immediately becomes frangible.

Right: Would you pay a lot more for a car with a drop-top, with a limited accommodation plan, and seating only two passenger doors? Hundreds did just that – buying Bentley or Rolls-Royce MPW models in the late 1960s.

Far right: This was the Rolls-Royce display at the Earls Court (London) motor show of 1971, when the Corniche was still a new model.

This, therefore, meant that coachbuilders would no longer be able to produce individual and exquisitely shaped Continentals, which had done so much to widen interest in Bentley during the 1950s and early 1960s. In fairness, as only two top-grade coachbuilders now remained – Mulliner Park Ward (a Rolls-Royce subsidiary), and James Young – it was easy to see who might suffer, and who might survive.

James Young tried to fight against the inevitable, by launching a two-door sedan version of these cars in 1965. Since the overall styling of their project was absolutely unaltered (one had to look hard, twice, and then very carefully, before realizing that there was only one door on each side) they proved to be unsuccessful. Only fifty such cars, fifteen of them badged as Bentleys, were ever sold. When that project closed down in 1967, the entire James Young business soon followed.

Rolls-Royce, in fact, had already thought this through, and had decided that it could afford to invest heavily in producing special two-door versions of its new unit construction body shell, by installing new

The Phantom VI of 1968, seen here with London's Houses of Parliament in the background, replaced the Phantom V. The change of title was accompanied by the use of a four headlamp nose, and by improved equipment. Such cars would go on to sell, slowly but steadily, into the 1990s.

After the two-door drop-head coupe was renamed Corniche in the 1970s, its style would be virtually unchanged for the next two decades. In this case, the registration plate – 20 TU – does not identify the date of manufacture, as it was a "personalized" number, which Rolls-Royce used repeatedly on its demonstrator cars.

press tools and body framing facilities at the Mulliner Park Ward factory in London, and by using Silver Shadow under frame/platforms as the basis for those new shells.

Although these were Rolls-Royce-designed cars, for the first few years they did not have a separate name, but were merely known as the "Mulliner Park Ward" cars. The sedan appeared in March 1966, and the convertible in September 1967, the two cars sharing many panels and inner structures. Pressed Steel supplied complete, though unpainted, welded-up Silver Shadow platforms to Willesden, and MPW did the rest. Because the platform was unchanged, and there was full four-seater accommodation, the general proportions were still the same – though almost all external panels (and many internal ones) were new. To save weight, the door shells, hood, and trunk lid assemblies were all crafted from aluminum alloy, and much reinforcement was made to the Silver Shadow-based underside, - principally to the tunnel and sills. When the convertible version came on stream, yet more stiffening was needed.

Once completed, the shells were transported to

Crewe to follow the four-door sedans through the newly established rustproofing, primer coating, painting and mechanical assembly processes, before being returned to Willesden for completion.

The new soft-top assembly itself had been totally engineering at MPW, who were true experts in this field. Naturally, it was electrically operated and, when stowed, it was stored in a snugly detailed fabric pouch around the rear seats. As Autocar pointed out in its description: "A reassuring safety factor is that the hood – electrically operated, together with the side windows – cannot be raised or powered unless the gear lever is in neutral and the handbrake in the "on" position."

These cars, incidentally, were always exclusive. When the MPW car was first revealed, Rolls-Royce claimed that it would be making 250 to 300 two-door cars every year (about 100 of which would be drop-heads). This was the limit of capacity at Willesden.

For the next few years, specification updates tracked those of the Silver Shadow sedans, though in some cases these cars were used to "shake down" new features also intended for the sedans. GM400 automatic transmission arrived on right-hand drive home market cars. It was fitted on two-door cars a few months (and 500 chassis) before the four-doors, as were the latest air-

Left: The Silver Shadow II was available from 1977, with a modified front-end style, including a squatter radiator shape, an underbumper spoiler, sleeker bumpers and (on later models) headlamp wipers.

Right: Compared with the original type, the nose of the Silver Shadow II had been cleaned up, with no auxiliary air intakes, and with no bumper over-riders. The profile, though, remained unmistakeable.

Below: The longer wheelbase Silver Shadow became known as the Silver Wraith II in 1977, and was available with or without a glass division between front and rear components. This car has the division, showing that the bench seat mechanism surrounding it was bulky.

Though its wheelbase had been stretched, the Silver Wraith II, complete with vinyl roof and more space in the rear compartment, was still a very elegant machine.

conditioning (six months and about 1,200 chassis), suspension changes, and other more minor details. The increase in engine capacity, however, came at the same time – autumn 1970 – as for the sedans.

During the winter months of 1970/1971, the two-door "Mulliner Park Ward" cars were caught up in the financial trauma of February 1971. The cars that took over from them (charismatically badged as "Corniche" models) were the first models to be launched after that fateful period.

Although Rolls-Royce's plunge into receivership in February 1971 was startling enough, the launch of new Corniche models immediately afterward was unprecedented. In a financial crisis, after all, one would expect economies, not the launch of exotic new products. The Cars Division, however, knew what it was doing, and merely had to convince the receiver of its strategy.

In reality there was less to the Corniche than met the eye, for in all of its most important respects, it was no more than a slightly reworked and more powerful Mulliner Park Ward two-door model. There was,

however, a new style of facia/instrument panel, complete with a tachometer, a special center console, and a three-spoke wood-rimmed 15-inch steering wheel, plus slightly different road-wheel trims.

In the next few years the Corniche sold steadily, and profitably, with few visual changes. Most technical innovations for sedans were first used on these two-door cars. No "sheet-metal" changes were ever made. In early 1977, the Corniche was mechanically updated in

line with the newly announced Silver Shadow II four-door sedans. More engine changes were going to be needed in the future. California cars were equipped with Bosch K-Jetronic fuel injection for the 1980 model year. In 1979 (this was never announced publicly) the Corniche and Camargue both got new-generation Silver Spirit rear suspension.

By this time, however, the Corniche sedan was overshadowed by the convertible version, so from the

Above: The Silver Shadow II, built from early 1977 to the summer of 1980, had a slightly modified front end style, power-assisted rack and pinion steering, the split level air-conditioning first seen in the Camargue, and a host of other detail improvements.

Left: This brand new fascia layout, which hid a complex split-level air conditioning installation, was fitted to all Camargues, and would be used in the Silver Shadow II/Bentley T2-Series from 1977. The same basic layout would then be carried forward into the next generation Silver Spirit/Mulsanne range of the 1980s.

Announced in 1975, the new Camargue coupe was the first Rolls-Royce to be shaped by Pininfarina, who always insisted that they would have done an even better job if they had been allowed to modify the famous radiator. One of the famous supersonic Concorde aircraft completes the backdrop.

fall of 1980 it was gradually phased out. After that, the company only built open-top Corniches, which were a continuing success. A total of 1,212 "pre-Corniche" cars (both identities) had already been built before 1971, and 1,171 Corniche saloons had followed during the 1970s, while many more convertibles than that had already been made.

Though 389 Corniches were produced in 1981, the company made a strategic decision, to rejuvenate the Bentley badge, and to make those cars progressively different from the Rolls-Royce machines on which they were based. Accordingly, in mid-1984, the Bentley Corniche was renamed the Bentley Continental. In the next decade no fewer than 441 Continentals (eight of them with Bentley Turbo turbocharged engines, to special order) would be built.

Amazingly, the Corniche/Continental models would stay in production throughout the 1980s and into the 1990s, reflecting the Silver Spirit's running gear changes, but retaining their unique style. So many changes, in name as well as in running gear, were made that these are listed:

For 1981, Bosch fuel injection was standardized on Corniches delivered to every state in the United States. From mid-1984, the Bentley version of this car was re-named "Continental," with a new fascia design. For 1986, Bosch fuel injection was standardized for all markets. And in the same year American market cars became Corniche II: these cars had ABS brakes, and new interiors, and were available in the UK from late 1987.

More was to follow. Corniche II became Corniche III in October 1989, with a new MK Motronic engine management system, and 6.5-inch, 15-spoke alloy wheels. At this time, Rolls-Royce claimed that the waiting list had stretched to three years. But that was before a worldwide recession struck, and sales halved. Because of the sudden sales collapse, Rolls-Royce closed the Willesden factory, relocating Corniche assembly to Crewe in 1992, with complete bare body shells supplied by Park Sheet Metal of Coventry.

The final model derivative – Corniche IV – appeared in 1991/1992, when Silver Spirit technology was added, including the use of the GM 4L80E transmission, active ride suspension, safety air bags, a heated rear window in the fold-back soft top, fascia changes and other improvements. The UK retail price at the end of 1991 was $238,000. In 1992, 25 Corniche IV "Anniversary" models commemorated the model name's 21st birthday – all cars being painted Ming Blue with a cream-colored soft top.

From August 1993, all Continental/Corniche types received V-8 engines which produced 20 per cent more power than before. Top speed rose to around 130 miles per hour. Finally, in August 1994, the company announced that Corniche assembly was soon to end, and the last batch of cars were all to be badged Corniche S.

The end finally came in summer 1995, after the Bentley Azure had gone on sale, when the very last Corniche was completed at Crewe. It was the last of a distinguished family of Bentley and Rolls-Royce cars, which had been on the market for 30 years, and which had sold in far higher numbers than any previous range to be built at Crewe.

In the meantime, in the mid-1970s, Rolls-Royce astonished everyone by launching a car that had not been styled in Britain, but in Italy. Until BMW took over in the 2000s, the Camargue was unique as the only Rolls-Royce production car ever to have been shaped by a foreign styling house. It was always controversial, and because only 530 such cars were built in eleven years, it is questionable whether it ever recouped its investment.

At the concept stage, although several rival cars were studied, reportedly it was the success of the front-wheel-drive Cadillac Eldorado coupe that caused such a stir at Crewe. By the time Rolls-Royce's "Delta" project got under way, it had become a "personal car," though one that would set every possible new standard – in price, specification, and market perception.

Although the first thoughts came along in 1968, there would not even be a single prototype on the road for another four years. The company elected to use the Silver Shadow platform and running gear in all, but to commission a new two-door coupe. Seeking an injection of styling expertise from outside, Pininfarina (and, in particular, Sergio Pininfarina, himself) was soon selected.

Rolls-Royce's brief to Pininfarina was broad-brush, but nevertheless constricting. The Silver Shadow/Corniche's platform and running gear had to be retained – with the same wheelbase, inner wheel arch, engine bay and basic floorpan/firewall panels all to be hidden away under a new skin. The result had to be a two-door coupe with four/five-seater accommodation.

At this time Rolls-Royce also decided to evolve a

complete new split-level air-conditioning system for its entire family of cars. This would first be seen in the Camargue, but would eventually be adapted to use in all other Silver Shadow-based cars, and even future models too.

Pininfarina's work was ready for approval by Rolls-Royce at the end of 1970, but then came Rolls-Royce's financial traumas of February 1971, and for a time every future product was thrown into confusion. However, because the car-building division was profitable, a go-ahead to make the first prototype followed in mid-1971.

The finalized Camargue shape had totally smooth sides, devoid of any styling gimmicks; the only decoration was a delicately profiled chrome strip along the flanks. It was a massive car, with the traditional grille erect – defiant even – on the nose. The Camargue was the same length as the Corniche, but four inches wider and about 245 pounds heavier. The latest package of Silver Shadow underpinnings, which included a wider rear track and fatter-section radial ply tires, was also standard on the new car.

To build the Camargue, Rolls-Royce had to work out how to complete the body shells. In the end, Pressed Steel supplied incomplete Silver Shadow platforms to the MPW works at Willesden, where craftsmen welded up the superstructure. Some panels came from MPW itself and some from outside suppliers. At first, there were great problems in producing satisfactory assemblies.

Completed shells were trucked to Crewe for rustproofing, prepaint work, and for most of the running gear to be installed. A part-finished Camargue would then be returned to Willesden for completion. This was a very long process, taking many weeks (up to six months on some cars). It goes without saying that every car was built to order, never for dealer stock.

When launched in the UK, no one could ignore the price, for at about $64,000 it was easily the most expensive production car on the British market. In 1975 this compared with about $42,000 for a Corniche sedan, or about $32,600 for a Silver Shadow. In other words you could buy two Silver Shadows for the price of one Camargue.

Deliveries began almost immediately, though U.S. customers had to wait until 1976. But because 390 Camargues eventually went to the United States, the American market became the savior of the project.

Although Camargues were on sale until 1986, production never even approached two cars a week. After the first 178 cars had been built at MPW, body shell assembly was moved to Motor Panels Ltd. of Coventry, in central England. Running gear was updated at the same time as its Corniche and Silver Shadow relatives.

Now that this car has gone, "classic" opinion about the Camargue is sharply divided. Those who understand what the Camargue project was all about see the need for a company flagship at that time, and recognize the strategy of giving the customer a wider choice. They also understood why it could never sell in large quantities.

During this period, incidentally, Rolls-Royce/Bentley production had surged ahead. In the mid-1960s, when the Silver Shadow family had been launched, no more than 1,500 cars left Crewe every year. By 1970, annual output had increased to 2,000, and by the end of the 1970s, it had leapt once again, this time to 3,300. That, in fact, was an all-time peak, for demand would fall away in the 1980s and 1990s.

Even so, when Rolls-Royce previewed the Silver Spirit range in its annual financial report of March/April 1980, the company had a lot of serious corporate strategy to analyze. The reason soon became clear – for in June it announced that it was to be taken over, amicably, by Vickers Ltd.,the giant British engineering conglomerate. This might have shocked Rolls-Royce enthusiasts – it was only seven years earlier that Rolls-Royce Motors Ltd had been floated on the stock market. But for financial observers it was an inevitable development.

The most recent company results had noted an annual turnover of $349 million, though pretax profits were down to $15.7 million. Because of the forecast effects of the second energy crisis, car sales and profits were likely to fall further in 1981. Rolls-Royce might not yet be in trouble, but if it was to continue to invest in new products – $55 million allocated to the new Silver Spirit was just the first new project planned for the 1980s – then larger financial reserves, or more heavyweight backing, was needed.

Chairman David Plastow insisted that no company had ever made a hostile approach, though other concerns had politely suggested that a merger might turn out well. In the end it was personal contact, and Plastow's charisma, that brought about the merger. Vickers, it seems, was not only looking to capture Rolls-Royce, but its top man – for Plastow became CEO of the entire Vickers Group in September 1980.

By then, it is worth noting that the Silver Shadow's price was an astonishing 640 per cent more than it had been in 1965 when originally launched. This, of course, was mainly due to the inflation, which raged in the UK during that period. In that time, sales had broken every possible Rolls-Royce record. Since 1965 30,057 Rolls-Royce saloons had been produced, along with 2,289 Bentley-badged examples - making 32,346 in all. Well over half of these cars had been sold to export markets, particularly to the U.S.

What happened to the two brands in the 1980s, though, showed just how fickle the automotive market could be.

CHAPTER Six

TURBOS & SPIRITS

ROLLS-ROYCE & BENTLEY IN THE 1980S & 1990S

ROLLS-ROYCE HAD TAKEN A LONG TIME TO DEVELOP A REPLACEMENT FOR THE LONG-RUNNING SILVER SHADOW/T-SERIES CARS. Even by the mid-1970s, a new model was on the stocks, though inside the company there was great controversy about the styling to be adopted. But, what was the hurry? As the existing cars were continuing to sell – annual sales actually increased, year after year, in the late 1970s – there seemed to be no rush to bring it to market.

Although management – engineers, certainly – would have liked to introduce a radically fresh model range, there were good financial reasons why this was never going to be possible. This, after all, was the period in which Bentley/Rolls-Royce was flying solo. It had only been floated on the stock market very recently, in 1973, and although the stock market was smiling indulgently at its corporate bravery, this did not mean that the company could afford to invest in an all-new car.

There was no question of that. The alternative solution was to engineer a new shape of car atop the existing platform and running gear and this would still cost an important proportion of the company's resources. In 1979, when investment in new tooling was at its height, the Rolls-Royce/Bentley combine's total turnover had been $211 million, yet the total investment in

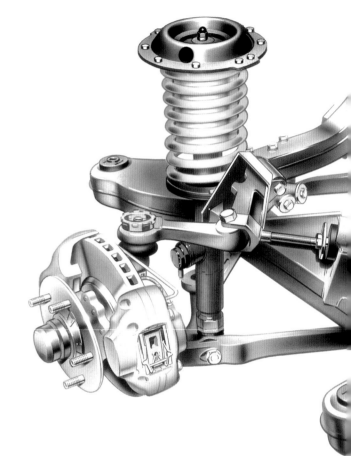

Above: First used under the Corniche/Camargue models in 1979 (but never advertised), and really intended for the Silver Spirit/Mulsanne cars, were modified indpendent suspensions.

Left: From the fall of 1980, there were two new, closely related, models from Crewe – the Rolls Royce Silver Spirit, and the Bentley Mulsanne. Both retained an updated version of the Silver Shadow/T-Series platform, but with this revised styling theme.

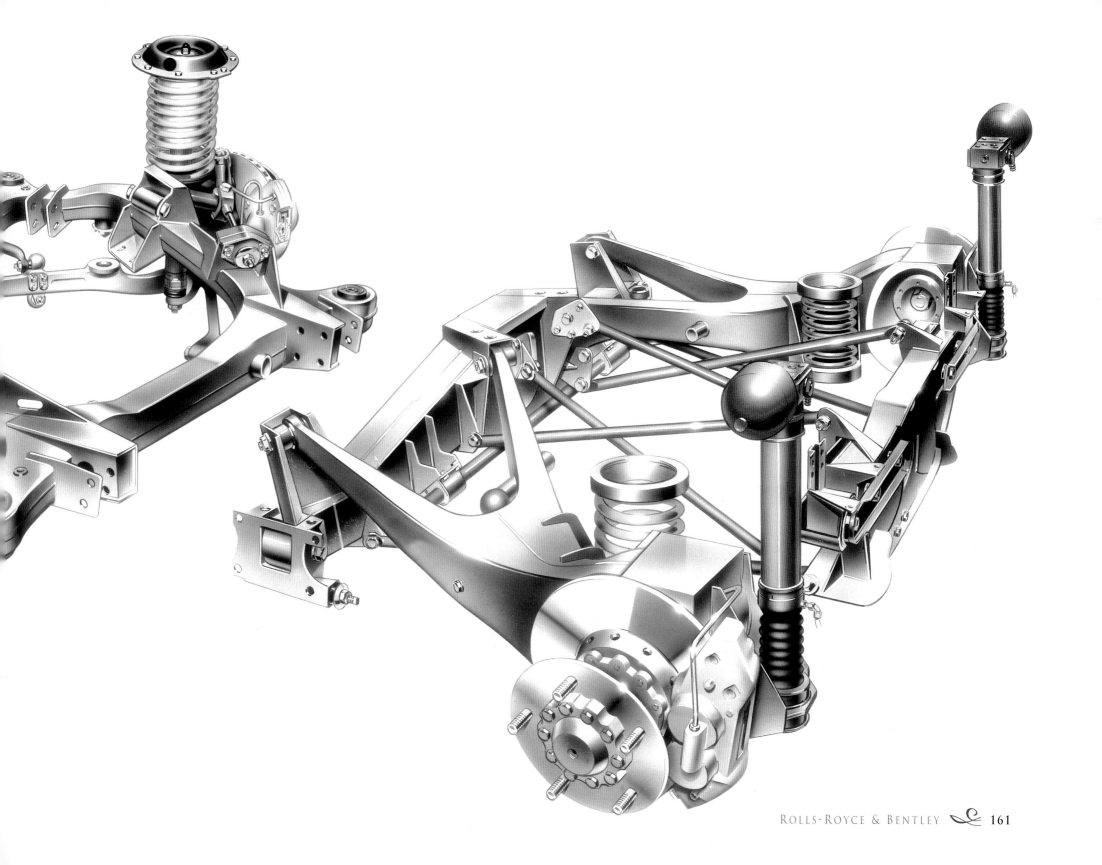

the new-type SZ generation was a creditable, but sizeable, $61.6 million. By the time Vickers took control in 1980 as the company's new owner, Rolls-Royce was in need of financial replenishment, which meant that Vickers's abundant capital reserves might prove to be very reassuring.

In the mid-1970s, therefore, Rolls-Royce had started work on a new range (this was coded SZ – the Silver Shadow generation had been SY), which took shape around the same basic platform and running gear as the well-established Silver Shadow. When the new cars arrived in 1980, it was no surprise that twin new models, Rolls-Royce Silver Spirit and Bentley Mulsanne, superficially looked like little more than reskinned versions of the old types.

Yet they were not. Much more than that had been involved. Above the floorpan, every body panel, and most of the body fittings, were new. The fact was, though, that the existing platform virtually defined the use of a conventional "three-box" layout, so stylist Fritz Feller's creation showed off the same basic proportions as before. The wheelbase had grown to 120.5 inches, but this was a mere detail, caused by the changes to the rear suspension, and the realignment of the semitrailing arms. The platform itself was not changed in that region. As ever with a modern Rolls-Royce, there was provision for standard-length and longer-wheelbase types, and as ever, it was company policy that there should be two different badges – Bentley and Rolls-Royce.

Although the company always insisted that it was even-handed in its promotion of both brands, by this time in the company's history the Bentley marque had certainly taken a back seat, and was virtually forgotten. Bentley enthusiasts, of course, had only themselves to blame, for the brand was always available. They could certainly have affected the balance by buying more of the cars!

The fact was that in 1980-1981 two differently badged cars – the Bentley Mulsanne and Rolls-Royce Silver Spirit – were being sold with identical technical specifications, near-identical styling, and at exactly the same retail price ($109,183 in the UK, at launch). In the first full year – 1981 – the company would sell just 151 Bentleys, but no fewer than 3,014 Rolls-Royces. This made no sense at all, so as a forward-looking business, the company had to do something about it.

It took time to make long-time strategic decisions, but after looking back into both the company's histories, and after studying the lush heritage, the company concluded that Bentley should once again be made to be as different from Rolls-Royce as was economically possible. Maybe not in styling, but in engineering, the differences began to pile up almost from that point. After all, by being "different" from Rolls-Royce (mechanically, if not in styling), Bentley had thrived from 1933 into the 1960s. It was only afterward, as the cars effectively became clones of each other, that Bentley's fortunes began to fade.

In the future, it was decided, Rolls-Royce and Bentley cars should gradually take on more and more of their own semi-independent characters. Although financial constraints would always be there (which meant that individual body styles, at least for the saloons, might never be justified), there was scope for changing, improving, and making the running gear more distinctive. Not only that, but when the time came to develop new two-door cars, these would be Bentleys, with no Rolls-Royce equivalents.

Accordingly, in the 1980s the Silver Spirit pedigree evolved only slowly – an ultralong wheelbase limousine arrived in 1984, and fuel-injected engines were

Above and right: A longer wheelbase version of the Silver Spirit, titled Silver Spur, was available from the very start of production in 1980 (above). Do you prefer the styling of the Silver Spirit (right) to the Silver Shadow which it replaced? For years, there was controversy within Rolls-Royce as to the merits of the new shape.

standardized in 1986, but that was about all. For Bentley, though, there were several big changes.

The new Bentley strategy evolved in two ways. On the one hand, the company developed a magnificent turbocharged model, the Mulsanne Turbo, and on the other it produced what we might now call an "entry-level" Bentley, the Eight, at a reduced price, but with very few reductions in equipment.

The Bentley Mulsanne family, launched in 1980, was to all intents and purposes a rebadged, reradiatored version of the Silver Spirit, with no more than cosmetic changes to justify the brand changes. Most cars had chrome-plated radiators, but this type, the Turbo, had a painted shell to flag up the differences.

Except for its painted radiator grille (right), it was almost impossible to tell the Mulsanne Turbo of the 1980s from its less powerful stable mates. Anyone who dared to open the hood of the original Mulsanne Turbo was confronted with a mass of machinery (above) – including the magic word "Turbo" atop the intake plenum. The 6.75-liter engine produced nearly 300 horsepower at this time.

It was the 300 horsepower Turbo, which caused such a stir in 1982. A few years later when the Turbo R model appeared, this added better road holding to the startling straight line performance, making it into more of a "driver's car." Although there would be much more detail improvement in the years that followed, this was the family of 1980s/1990s-style Bentleys that the clientele flocked to buy.

First with the Turbo, then with the Turbo R, and finally with a series of special two-door cars that were developed from them, Bentley's image and sales were transformed. By 1990 Bentley's annual sales matched those of Rolls-Royce, and by the mid-1990s Bentley had quite outstripped its stable mate. In 1996, with preparations to launch a new model range going strongly ahead, Bentley would sell 1,235 cars, against a mere 509 from Rolls-Royce.

The next big technical leap forward came in the 1989

In late 1986 the turbocharged Bentley V-8 engine, for all markets, inherited a new Bosch fuel injection installation – and was rated at 328 horsepower. Bentley was proud of that – but there was more to follow in the 1990s.

When the turbocharged Bentley Mulsanne was upgraded in 1985, with cast alloy road wheels and a much firmer set of suspension settings, the result was the Bentley Turbo R (R = Roadholding). This was a far more sporting car than any previous Crewe-built Bentley, and helped to separate the image of the brand from Rolls-Royce itself.

– 1992 period. First, in 1989 Rolls-Royce introduced electronically controlled adaptive damping to its suspension system. (This firmed up the ride when the car was being driven hard, softening it off for town driving or constant-speed cruising). Next, in 1991/1992,

From 1984 the two-door drop-head coupe Bentley was renamed Continental – a famous model name of the 1950s and 1960s – though in almost every way it was a slightly improved Corniche. It would remain on sale for the next decade.

the company finally dropped the old GM400 automatic transmission in favor of a more modern development, the GM 4L80E four-speed automatic.

In the same period, Bentley's Mulsanne first became "S" and then, in 1992 both the Eight and the Mulsanne were dropped in favor of the Brooklands. In the meantime, in 1989 Bentleys had also been given a new "corporate" nose style, with four circular headlamps instead of the rectangular lamps, which it had previously shared with Rolls-Royce.

Bentley enthusiasts finally got the chance in 1991 to buy a new type of two-door car, though there would be no Rolls-Royce equivalent. In fact, the Corniche/Continental generation of two-door types had been around for so long that few expected them ever to be replaced – saloon and convertible since 1971, convertible only since that time.

Bentley had other ideas. Once enough investment capital could be allocated, they re-introduced a two-door coupe, the Continental R. It was like 1952, and the R-Type Continental, all over again. The first of a new line of coupes and convertibles was previewed at the Geneva Show in 1991.

Developed on the latest Mulsanne/Rolls-Royce Silver Spirit platform, the chassis and running gear –

Large, but elegant, the Bentley Continental R went on sale in 1991 as a full four-seater coupe, based on the platform and running gear of the contemporary Bentley Mulsanne/Rolls-Royce Silver Spirit platform.

including the 360 horsepower turbocharged V-8 engine – were derived from those of the Turbo R. The style, though, was completely new.

Initially, Bentley would introduce the new fixed-head coupe, though the ancient Continental convertible would continue alongside it for some time. That would finally retire in 1995, in favor of a new convertible to be called Azure. Finally, and to round out the range, there would be a full-on, ultra-high-performance, short-wheelbase version of the coupe, to be called the Continental T.

The new car's style took a few of its cues from the original R-Type, and there were definite similarities in the overall proportions. Both cars, of course, were two-door/four-seater fixed-head coupes – and by the standards of the day both were colossally fast.

Except for the new GM 4L80E transmission, other innovations were confined to the interior, and the furnishings. The fascia and full-length center console were entirely new, there was all-electric adjustment for the seats. The seats could be electrically warmed, and for the first time on a Bentley, the automatic transmission lever quadrant was placed in the center

Far left: *Although the Java drop-head coupe of 1994 was only a nonrunning prototype, it was fitted out just as carefully, and luxuriously, as any other Bentley production car.*

Left: By the 1990s, the stylist/designers had turned their attention to the engine bay of these cars – and specified this smart plastic shroud over the mass of manifolding, pipe-work and electrical connections of the big V-8 engine. Difficult to imagine, isn't it, that there was still a big engine underneath?

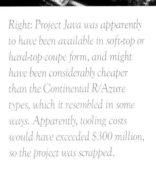

Right: Project Java was apparently to have been available in soft-top or hard-top coupe form, and might have been considerably cheaper than the Continental R/Azure types, which it resembled in some ways. Apparently, tooling costs would have exceeded $300 million, so the project was scrapped.

Far right: The Bentley Continental R, launched in 1991 was by any standards the sportiest Bentley to have gone on sale for a long time. Even though it only had two passenger doors, it was a full four-seater.

Right: No lack of information in the fascia/instrument display of the Bentley Continental R coupe, for this car had a sweeping new center console containing air conditioning, radio system, and electric seating adjustment controls. The steering had an air bag, and there was a tachometer, even though the big V-8 engine could rarely exceed 4,000 rpm.

Left: The Bentley Continental R made its bow in 1991, based on the existing platform and running gear as the Silver Spirit/Bentley Mulsanne family, but with a two-door/four-seater fixed-head coupe body style, a 330 horsepower engine and a top speed of around 150 miles per hour.

The fabulous Bentley Continental T, announced in 1996, was not only a shorter wheelbase version of the Continental (the wheelbase was reduced by 4 inches), but it had 18-inch wheels as standard, and no less than 400 horsepower. On special order, 440-horsepower-engined versions were also available.

Customers ordering a 155-mile per hour Continental T could either have the traditional wooden dashboard, or this extra-special tooled aluminium fascia.

console.

Even though the new Continental R cost $256,000, seventy cars were built in 1991, 146 in 1992, 285 in 1993, and 251 in 1994 – a rate that settled at about six cars a week, enough to keep Bentley (and Park Sheet Metal of Coventry, who supplied body shells) busy. Final assembly was always at Crewe.

In the meantime, work went ahead on the new-type convertible, which appeared in 1995, badged as the Bentley Azure. Although the basic style and seating package was like that of the Continental R, there was more innovation.

It had not been simple to chop off the roof and substitute a fold-back soft top. The Italian styling house,

Pininfarina, had spent more than two years evolving the electrically powered fold-back mechanism. The Italians were eventually contracted to produce complete body shells, from under pans and sub assemblies supplied from Park Sheet Metal.

This was a complex and lengthy business, reflected in the original price ($344,000), for Pininfarina also had to add considerable under-floor stiffening to compensate for the loss of rigidity inflicted by chopping off the roof. After completing the bare shells, Pininfarina also painted them, and added the folding soft-top mechanism, before returning the ensemble to Crewe. More than 250 cars were built in the first full twelve-month period.

The most extrovert Bentley so far, the Continental T, then appeared in 1996. In effect, the Continental T was no more than a shorter-wheelbase Continental R: the 4.5-inch chop reduced the cabin length, and rear seat space.

Turbocharged V-8 engine power continued to rise during this period – 385 horsepower on the Azure and now 400 horsepower on the Continental T – while the rear wheel arches were flared to accept super-fat 18-inch

To bring the turbocharged Bentley story to its logical conclusion, Turbo R became Turbo RT in 1997, with no important style changes, but with its engine boosted to no less than 400 horsepower

Here is the Bentley Azure of 1995. Think of a Continental R with its roof chopped off, then equipped with a beautifully detailed power-operated soft top engineered by Pininfarina. The Italian firm also took control of part of the production process, so considerably travel costs were involved. No wonder the original UK price was $344,000 - $59,000 more than the last of the Continental types.

tires. The ride height was reduced, and the ride was much harder than on other cars in this model group. This time, too, there was a choice between polished wood, or a milled alloy metal finish to the fascia/dashboard paneling. This was a thunderously fast, extrovert and effective car that could reach 170 miles per hour.

Although Bentley thought that only 40 of these hand-crafted coupes might be sold in a year, 133 cars were sold in the 1997 model year. This rate – two to three deliveries every week – subsequently stabilized.

Even after the takeover of Bentley by VW, there was time for a further derivative to be launched, the Continental SC (SC = Sedanca Coupe), where the roof of the Continental R was revamped to provide

Below: Reviving a famous (Bentley) name, by applying it to a Rolls-Royce, the Flying Spur of 1994 not only had the longer-wheelbase body shell of the previous Silver Spur, but was the very first turbocharged Rolls-Royce, for it had the 330-horsepower engine of the contemporary Bentley Turbo R.

Above: In the Flying Spur of the 1900s, even the air conditioning and sound system control panels of the center console were carefully and elegantly worked out.

Customers with a lot of spare money could use the Special Commission Bentley service to make their cars even more individual. The special features might not only include a maximum-output, 440-horsepower engine, but might also include different colour schemes, fittings, and extras. The only obvious "Special" fitting on this car, from the outside, are the chrome-plated door mirrors and the brightwork finish of the 18-inch road wheels.

detachable Targa-style panels.

These, though, were the last – the very last – of the traditional Bentleys, and the miracle was that they survived into the new century. Price listed until 2003,

the season in which the new VW-based Bentley went into full production, they were the last survivors of the old T-Series/Mulsanne generation.

By that time, in any case, there had been major

technical and managerial changes at Crewe. In the run-up to the launch of a new model range, the company had rung the changes in its saloon/limousine range in every possible way. During the 1990s, not only did

The Bentley Continental SC (SC stood for Sedanca Coupe, and there was no Rolls-Royce equivalent) was the very exclusive half-way house between a Continental R or Continental T (permanent fixed-head coupes) and the Azure (full continental). The engineering and style allowed the front roof panel to be removed, 'Targa' style, but the rear cabin sections were fixed.

Rolls-Royce reintroduce famous old names like Flying Spur and Silver Dawn, but there were also several new variations on the long-wheelbase limousine theme. (The Park Ward limousine, introduced in 1996, was the final iteration). Not only that, but from 1994 the Flying Spur and Silver Spur types were powered by turbocharged engines – the first time such an engine had ever been used on a Rolls-Royce automotive engine.

Number crunchers analyzing this period need to tread very carefully, for a torrent of model names were used in the 1980 – 1998 period. No fewer than 26 different Bentleys and 22 different Rolls-Royce models

The Continental SC, based on the shorter wheelbase Continental T structure, was a fabulously rare beast. It had the Sedanaca Coupe body arrangements, which allowed the front roof panel to be removed (as shown) or for it to be re-fixed when bad weather threatened.

all ran on the same basic platform. Some of them are extremely rare, such as the one-off Bentley Camargue of 1985 and the three turbocharged Bentley Continentals of 1992.

Two decades later, however, an engineering revolution was finally on the horizon, and the days of the Mulsanne generation were already numbered. The year 1998 would be a time of great change.

The evolution of a new range of Rolls-Royces and Bentleys was influenced by the corporate upheavals, which seemed to occupy much of the 1990s. The new cars that appeared in 1998 were very different from those tentatively planned in the 1980s. In almost every way – construction, the engines to be used, and the marketing approach – they changed completely along the way.

It was the ownership of the Rolls-Royce/Bentley business that was central to all this. In 1983, when the first ideas took shape, Rolls-Royce and Bentley were controlled by Vickers. By the early 1990s, when development began in earnest, the Rolls-Royce aircraft engine giant (Rolls-Royce PLC), which still controlled trade mark rights to the Rolls-Royce name, had started an aircraft engine joint project with BMW of Germany.

Even so, it was soon clear that the company could no longer afford to design, develop and manufacture a brand new engine of its own. Therefore, for the first time in a long corporate history, a search began to buy engines from another company. Ideally that company should be European, and it should not be a direct rival, but the power units would have to be of the highest quality.

By 1994 the search had narrowed down to a choice between BMW and Mercedes-Benz – both highly prestigious German concerns. At the end of 1994, Mercedes-Benz was favored, but BMW was finally chosen. (This caused Mercedes-Benz to take offence in

the strongest possible way.) Everything was settled – or so it seemed.

The Silver Spirit had only been on sale for three years when work started on its eventual replacement. Mike Dunn (ex-Ford, whose father had been technical director of Alvis for some years) became the new technical director. He was tasked with inspiring the birth of a totally new model range.

It was always certain that a new car would have an

The back seat of the "Targa"-roofed Bentley Continental SC was fitted out with two individual chairs. There seemed to more glass than metal in the roof.

entirely new unit construction monocoque. And it would have to be more energy-efficient than the Silver Spirit/Mulsanne – a lighter car if possible, just as powerful but more fuel-efficient than before, and with a more wind-cheating style. In fact the twin new models – called Bentley Arnage and Rolls-Royce Silver Seraph – were not finally ready for launch until the spring of 1998, when the company sell-off dramas were at their height.

Vickers' decision to sell off the combined Rolls-

Bentley or Rolls-Royce? At this stage in the prototype-testing phase, in the searing weather of the Arizona desert, it made no difference. This picture dates from 1996.

Above: By the 1990s, the Silver Spirit had received a full decade of development, with better suspension, fuel-injected V-8 engines, and more (unstated) power than ever before. The Silver Spirit II arrived in 1989 and this version, the Silver Spirit III, followed in 1994. There were no important style changes, for all the advances were hidden away.

Left: The British registration number of this 1998 model Arnage – 1 WO – reminded everyone that it was Walter Owen Bentley ("WO" to all his fans, past and present) who had founded this brand in the first place. The only styling difference between this car and the Silver Seraph was in the grille.

Royce and Bentley business was finance oriented, rather than a product oriented. As fate would have it, it brewed up while the new-generation cars were approaching launch. It happened too late to influence the form of the new cars, but its fallout would have a lasting effect on both brands.

Stylistically, the only difference between the Rolls-Royce Silver Seraph and the Bentley Arnage was the front grille. This car, naturally, is a Silver Seraph.

Right: The shape, layout, and general ambience of fascia from Crewe changed only slowly. This was a 1998 Rolls-Royce Silver Seraph, complete with steering wheel that included an air-bag, which had definite artistic roots in the panels seen in earlier models of the 1970s and 1980s. Wood, leather, and high-quality carpet, of course, were all there, in abundance.

Below: The Rolls-Royce Silver Seraph of 1998 was powered by a normally aspirated 5.4-liter BMW V-12 engine. This was an engine already in use in BMW 7-Series cars – and it was the first outside engine ever to be used in a Rolls-Royce.

For those reasons, a short analysis, titled "Running Battle," is presented on page 206.

Cleverly, but invisibly, the engineers had packaged the same new body to accept two totally different BMW engines. The Rolls-Royce Silver Seraph would use a 5.4-liter V-12 engine, with two valves per cylinder, single overhead-camshaft heads, and 322 horsepower. The Bentley Arnage, though, would use a 350 horsepower, 4,398cc V-8, with twin overhead camshafts and four valves per cylinder, thanks to a twin turbocharging development that had been carried out by Cosworth. The Bentley would sell for some $16,000 less than the equivalent Rolls-Royce.

Here were two closely related new cars that were a quantum leap ahead of the old-generation Silver Spirit/Mulsanne types, which they were to replace. Although just as large as before – in fact, the new car was five inches longer, rode on a two-inch longer wheelbase, and weighed an extra 188 pounds – they looked smaller and somehow less ponderous.

Details included making the radiator shell less prominent, and making every panel softer in its profile and proportions. The interior packaging was virtually the same as that of the outgoing sedan, the interior being trimmed, finished, and presented in the same ageless manner. This time around, too, stylists made sure that the Rolls-Royce had a fascia/instrument layout quite different from that of the Bentley "sister" car.

The new engines put their power through a ZF five-speed automatic transmission, the ensemble riding in a new chassis/structure, which was claimed to be 65 per cent stiffer than the old shell. Suspension was all-independent, with a new layout featuring coil springs and wishbones at each end of the car.

In both cases, the long-established character of the twin marques had changed completely. Previous models had used low-revving, high-torque power units, ideally matched to their transmissions, and incredibly easy to drive. Now, they would be powered by high-revving, high-tech power units that announced their presence a little more obviously. They were, in effect, becoming more like other cars, rather than unique in what they offered. They were still great cars, but different. But would the clientele to be convinced?

The new cars were different in several other ways. Body shells would be assembled at Crewe, using panels and subassemblies provided by specialist press shops. Additionally, they would be put together on a moving assembly line. The "moving track," by the way, crept along at a snail-like 0.01 mile per hour – about 140 yards

Both new types went on sale in 1998, but it was the Bentley Arnage (with its turbocharged V-8 engine) that got most of the attention. Here it is, posed outside buildings at the famous Le Mans 24 Hour race circuit in France.

in a day – which was just long enough to see one Silver Seraph/Arnage travel the length of the assembly hall.

The twin new models got off to a very slow start, for several reasons. One was that the company wanted to be absolutely sure that they were being built correctly, and another was that the order book took time to fill, as the clientele were reluctant to take to the new models at first. They had to be weaned away from big, slow-revving V-8s, to the high-revving, high-tech, BMW engines.

Although the V-12-engined Silver Seraph would carry on until 2002, the new owners put less and less marketing effort behind the car. Two more new models would follow – a new-type Corniche and a long-wheelbase Park Ward limousine – but the Rolls-Royce brand effectively marked time until BMW took it over, as agreed, at the end of 2002.

Sales figures bear this out. Although the Silver Seraph was perhaps the most sophisticated, and certainly the fastest and most silent, of any Rolls-Royce built since World War II – it lacked promotion. Because VW effectively left the car to wither on the vine, it eventually died of neglect. A total of 442 Rolls-Royces were sold in 1999 (the first full year), 352 in 2001, and only 147 in the last "Crewe" year of 2002.

The only "new" Rolls-Royce to appear under VW ownership was the new generation Corniche convertible, which went on sale early in 2000. This car was quite clearly derived from the Bentley Azure, and obviously was conceived well before Vickers sold off the brand to VW.

Amazingly, it went on sale two years after the new Arnage. Like the Bentley Azure, it ran on an old-type Silver Spirit/Mulsanne/Turbo R platform, suspension, and running gear, complete with the old-type "Bentley," as opposed to the "BMW" V-8 engine. The engine itself was derated to 325 horsepower (the Azure engine produced 385 horsepower), and although the

From 1998 there was a very slow-moving assembly line at Crewe – a modern feature that had never before been seen in this historic factory. But before it could all be brought together, the careful "mating" of front and rear subframes with the body shell had to be perfected in static conditions. And with a truckload of machinery like that – that is a twin-turbocharged V-8 engine ready to go into an Arnage engine bay – there was no room for mistakes.

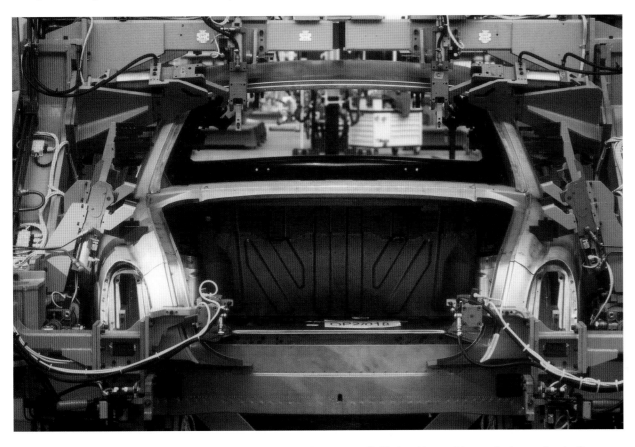

For production of the Rolls-Royce Silver Seraph/Bentley Arnage cars, Rolls-Royce installed body welding and framing facilities within the Crewe works. This was the first time that all-steel bodies had been fashioned at Crewe.

Above: Folding the power-operated soft top of the Arnage Drop Head Coupe was a complicated business, and of course it reduced the trunk storage space considerably.

Far right: No sooner had Rolls-Royce unveiled the new-type Corniche, than Bentley revealed the Arnage Drop head coupe, which had exactly the same type of two-door DHC body style, but with the 450-horsepower engine.

Right: Wall-to-wall burl walnut and a full display of instruments and controls were a familiar feature of the Bentley Arnage Drop Head Coupe. This was a full four-seater car, of course.

Rolls-Royce was very adept at mixing and matching models, platforms, styles, and model names. In 2000 a new-type Corniche was introduced – it would only be on sale for two years. This effectively was the Rolls-Royce version of the Bentley Azure, with the same basic two-door drop-head coupe style, modified with a Rolls-Royce nose incorporating Silver Seraph-type headlamps. The 6³/4-liter V-8 engine was less powerful than that of the Azure, with "only" 325 horsepower, and a claimed top speed of 135 miles per hour.

convertible body shape was clearly an iteration of the Azure shell itself, the nose was definitely related to the new Silver Seraph, and Rolls-Royce insisted that most of the skin panels were different from those of the Azure.

Like the old-type Corniche, this was not meant to be a sports car. With a top speed of 135 miles per hour,

however, there was a lot of performance to enjoy. It was a full four-seater, sumptuously equipped, convertible, complete with a vast, complex, electrically powered soft top. As *Autocar's* Steve Cropley wrote when he drove a car in California: "It does not drive, it glides . . . with its new, stiffer, body and remarkably quiet progress through the air, the Corniche brings new levels of

refinement to open-topped cruising . . . In the right circumstances – scenery, balmy weather, sparsely trafficked roads, time to spare – it is completely intoxicating . . ."

It was, in other words, an open-top Rolls-Royce in the best tradition of the marque – but because of the political situation surrounding its launch, it would only be on sale until 2002, becoming one of the rarest modern Rolls-Royce cars.

What VW called the "Last of Line Series" Seraph, mechanically standard with its BMW V-12 engine, but decked out in two-tone paintwork, with rosewood burl woodwork in the cabin, was introduced in August 2001. Only 170 of those cars, it was said, would be built – but it took a whole year for them to trickle through the assembly halls. The last of them left Crewe in August 2002, after which the brand went into hibernation for the winter.

Bentley, therefore, would be dominant in the 1998-2002 period, though it had its own traumas and its own dramas along the way. The fact is that the clientele did not take to the new BMW-engined Arnage at all, and within weeks they made their preference for the old-type V-8 engine very clear indeed.

Amazingly, Bentley listened, agreed with their demands, was able to complete a V-8 engine-swap project in double-quick time (even though this strategy had never been considered when the body hull was laid out). Bentley installed a twin-turbo derivative of the ancient $6\frac{1}{2}$-liter V-8 engine, and put the Arnage Red

Announced in 2000, the Silver Seraph "Park Ward" model had a 10-inch longer wheelbase, and the extra space in the rear compartment was obvious. This type of car could have a variety of extra equipment fitted, the space between the rear seats being an ideal place to add a "communications centre."

One of the last new-model Rolls-Royces to be announced at Crewe was the "Park Ward" sedan model, which had a 10-inch wheelbase stretch over the Silver Seraph, intended to make the rear seat more spacious. Rolls-Royce thought it might sell up to 60 cars a year of this type, though the last was produced in 2002.

Far elft: The only way to tell an Arnage Red Label from the earlier type was by observing the fatter tyres on 18-inch road wheels, and by spying the actual red label background to the Bentley badge on the nose. This was never going to be easy on such a fast car.

Left: This as the fascia/instrument panel display of the Arnage Red Label, as announced at the end of 1999. Bentley saw no reason why ultrahigh performance should not be delivered in great comfort, style, and refinement.

Left: The Bentley customer of the late 1990s and early 2000s Bentley customer could have all manner of special equipment added to his new car before delivery. This was the craftsman-built rear compartment of an Arnage Red Label, as exhibited at the Paris Motor Show.

Label on the market before the end of 1999. By previous Rolls-Royce Bentley standards, that was a sensationally rapid turn-around. Although the company has never admitted to anything, many pundits think that such a project was planned even before the original Arnage was unveiled.

From that moment, Bentley's image began to recover, as "VW-Bentley" gradually improved and expanded the Arnage range. The BMW-engined version was discreetly dropped in 2000, only two years after the first production car had been delivered, after which all Bentley road cars reverted to their traditional type of V8 power.

Because VW now concentrated on its hard-won Bentley marque (and left Rolls-Royce to fend for itself), it meant that the traditional expansion of the range all came behind the Bentley radiator. After the Arnage Red Label came the Arnage R. Then in 2002 there was the Arnage T, with no less than 450 horsepower, and a 400 horsepower long-wheelbase "Mulliner" limousine was also launched at the end of 2002.

Not only that, but early in 2005 Bentley also showed the prototype of a car called the Arnage Drophead Coupe, which had a 450-horsepower version of the V-8 engine, and whose style/structure harked back to the

Left: When developing the Arnage T model, Bentley engineers reworked the venerable old V-8 engine, with twin turbochargers (one feeding each cylinder bank) so that peak power rose to 450 horsepower. This was the most ever achieved from this slow-revving power unit.

Below: Because there was no flamboyant badging at the rear of the Arnage T, the only way that it could be identified was by the twin oval section exhaust tail pipes.

Right: The Arnage T was a massively powerful 450 horsepower car, with the twin-turbocharger engine, and special wheels to emphasise the high-performance image.

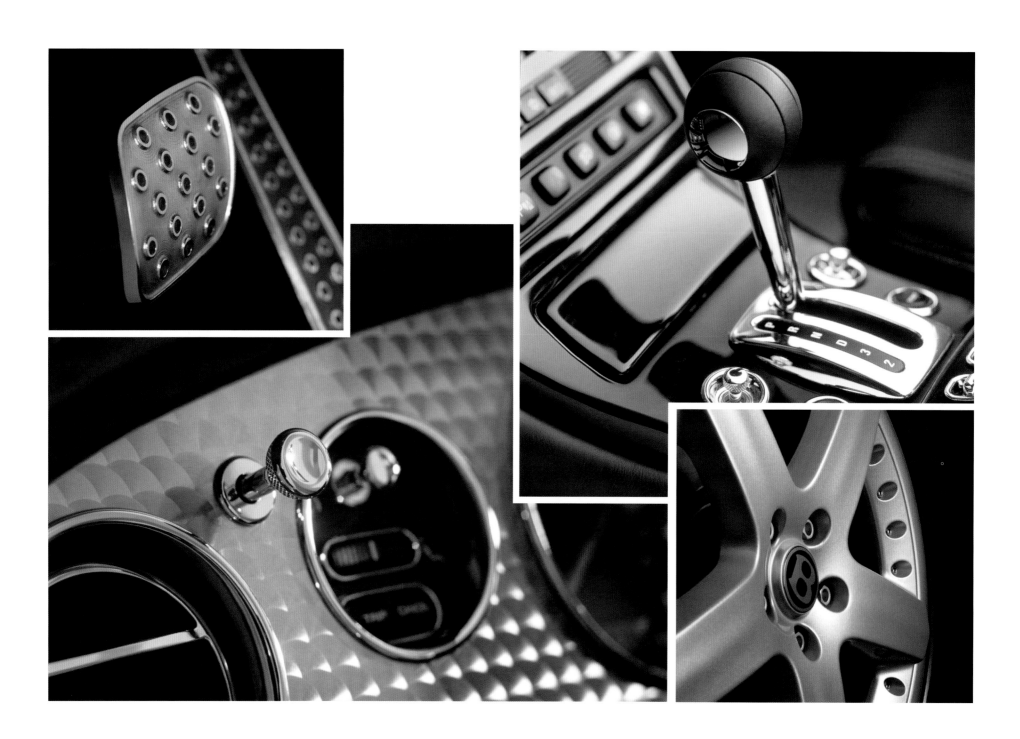

Queen Elizabeth broke with fifty years of tradition in 2002 by acquiring a Bentley state limousine instead of a Rolls-Royce. This magnificent machine, which rolled on a 151.3-inch wheelbase, with a 400-horsepower 6-liter Bentley V-8 engine, used a much-stretched Arnage Red Label platform, though the rest of the seven-seater body was entirely special. It went into service in time for the queen's Golden Jubilee celebrations. It became her "front line" machine, and is likely to remain so for at least the next twenty years.

Azure, by way of the 2000-2002 model Rolls-Royce Corniche. If the demand was there, Bentley told the world, then they would put this car on the market.

In 2002, however, the company revealed a new Bentley that would definitely not go on sale – for this was a stunning, one-off state limousine for Queen Elizabeth. This was a real break with tradition.

For a full half-century, every new British "royal" car had been a Rolls-Royce limousine – but now, for the very first time, the queen took delivery of a new Bentley state limousine. This had been built on behalf of the SMMT (the British Society of Motor Manufacturers and Traders), as a Golden Jubilee present to commemorate her first fifty years on the throne. It was immediately nicknamed "Betty's New Barge" (not within royal hearing).

Although there was a fleet of Rolls-Royce limousines in the Royal Mews, it was ageing fast, for the queen's last new car dated from 1987. To allow the oldest examples to be retired, a new Royal Limousine was overdue. Engineered for a possible life of 25 years and 125,000 miles, the new Bentley was capable of an (electronically limited) 125 miles per hour, but might also spend much time creeping along at only 10 miles per hour, and sometimes at walking pace.

The SMMT commissioned a new Bentley in 2000. Bentley then put much effort into reengineering the Arnage Red Label chassis and structure into a much bigger and heavier limousine. Incidentally, this was the first ever royal limousine to be built on the basis of a monocoque structure.

The result was a motorcar not only 32-inches longer than a standard Arnage, but 3,086 pounds heavier than the standard car. That weight increase was so colossal that many assumed that some protective armor plating had also been included, though this was not confirmed.

Among the details was the ability of the V-8 engine to run on Liquid Petroleum Gas, and there was a larger alternator to cope with added demands of the electrical installation.

Although recognizably derived from the Arnage, this limousine was bulkier, considerably higher, and with a great deal more space in the rear compartment. It was built by 34 craftsmen at Bentley Mulliner at Crewe, all of whom later signed a commemorative plate, which was fixed inside the body shell.

Special light tinted glass was fitted all round, with specially up-rated air conditioning. In the end, not only Bentley, but Mayflower (for the sheet metal bodywork), TWR (for the trim packaging) and Ricardo (power

train development) were all involved in what was a complex project.

Inside the car, naturally, there was a glass division between the front and rear compartments, and the rear was equipped with what were effectively separate seats, each of which could be raised so that the Royal occupants could see – and be seen – with ease.

The new state limousine caused quite a stir, for its first official outing was to take the queen and the duke of Edinburgh to and from St Paul's Cathedral for the Jubilee National Service of Thanksgiving on June 4, 2002. There would be many such trips in the years to come.

By 2002, however, VW had made it clear that the traditional type of Bentley was now living on borrowed time. Although existing Arnage and Arnage-related models would continue for the time being, the future would lie in VW-based products. Previews of the new Continental GT Coupemade clear what they meant by that.

Running battle: Rolls-Royce and Bentley for sale. Who bought the brands?

In October 1997, when Vickers decided to sell off the Rolls-Royce/Bentley automobile manufacturing business, it should have been a straightforward operation. That was the theory, but that was not the way things happened. By the time the dust of a very messy takeover battle had settled, and Vickers had netted some $770 million, several corporate egos had been seriously damaged, and the two marques had gone to different homes. The complication was that BMW already had a long-term contract to supply engines for the about-to-be-launched Silver Seraph/Arnage range, and that Rolls-Royce would effectively become an orphan for the next five years.

Two huge German concerns, BMW and VW, were interested in buying the business, and would eventually come to corporate blows over this. (Daimler-Benz was still miffed at losing the engine supply deal in 1994.) BMW (which already had aircraft engine commercial links with Rolls-Royce PLC, the separate aircraft engine building concern) was the initial favorite. VW eventually stepped in, and offered a higher price. Vickers, characteristically, then dithered, and the skies clouded over.

Although VW was mainly interested in Bentley and its sporting possibilities, BMW was drawn toward Rolls-Royce. When VW looked like winning, BMW pointed out its engine supply contract, and threatened to pull the plug on that deal.

Even so, when Vickers accepted VW's $770 million bid in June 1998, the fight appeared to be over – but it wasn't. BMW approached its friendly aerospace partner, Rolls-Royce PLC, for support. Rolls-Royce PLC subsequently confirmed that it still held the rights, in law, to decide on the use of the "Rolls-Royce" trademark – and that it wanted those transferred to BMW.

VW had no answer to this. Several top-level meetings between the two German companies took place, and in the end a very untidy, and demeaning, compromise was concluded in July 1998. VW took control of Bentley, the factory at Crewe, all its facilities, staff, and existing projects. VW also agreed to carry on manufacturing Rolls-Royce cars, including new models already under development, until 2002, though that brand was discreetly allowed to wither on the vine. By 2002, though, VW would have pumped millions into Crewe to reequip its facilities, and would introduce an all-new, VW/Audi-based range of Bentleys – the Continental GT and Flying Spur types. Sales, they forecasted, would surge to over 5,000 a year before long.

BMW, for its part, agreed that the current (Silver Seraph) generation of Rolls-Royce cars should be built alongside Bentleys at Crewe until the end of 2002, and that they would honor the already-signed engine supply deal up to that time. BMW also paid some $65 million for the automotive rights to the Rolls-Royce name. From January 1, 2003, however, they would have unfettered rights to market Rolls-Royce, and would relaunch it according to their own wishes. These, incidentally, were that a new model would be based on BMW engineering, and that it would be assembled at a brand new factory at Goodwood, in Sussex. This site was actually on the famous Goodwood estate, close to Goodwood House, and to the one-time motor racing circuit.

Although none of the businesses, or brands involved, came out of this tussle without bruises, both famous brands survived the holocaust, and both appeared to have good prospects as the 2000s developed.

Incidentally, only 15 months after it had sold out, Vickers itself was taken over – by Rolls-Royce PLC, the aircraft engine giant. The price of $933 million was little more than it had received for the two famous automotive brands, and for the real estate that went with them. So, in some ways, the wheel had come full circle.

CHAPTER *Seven*

BENTLEY UNDER VW

A COMPLETE MARKETING REVOLUTION

VW TOOK LONGER TO GET TO GRIPS WITH BENTLEY, and the business that it had so acrimoniously taken over, than had originally been planned. By the time all the infighting that decided the fate of the Rolls-Royce brand had been ended, it was the summer of 1998. Then, and only then, could VW start to sort out the corporate mess, to start putting Rolls-Royce on to a "care-and-maintenance" basis, and to start planning properly for Bentley's future.

The Bentley Arnage Limousine, announced in 2003, had a 28.66-inch longer wheelbase than the normal production Arnage sedan. It had that car's doors, but with a large fixed panel between them; front and rear body sections, proportions, and structures were like those of the saloon. Prices were settled by the amount of extra equipment ordered when the car was being produced at Crewe but, in the UK it would cost about $650,000 to put one on the road.

From that moment, in effect, VW wanted little more to do with Rolls-Royce. Although it halted the development of major new models, it was sensible enough to finalize the Rolls-Royce Corniche Convertible and put that on sale. In the meantime, it began to seriously concentrate its efforts on the Bentley brand.

In future, when special coach built conversions or stretched limousine evolutions were proposed, these would normally have Bentley identities (a first at Crewe). When the British SMMT (Society of Motor Manufacturers and Traders) decided to buy a new state limousine to present to Queen Elizabeth for her Golden Jubilee, it thus became a Bentley. The car broke new ground by being the very first Bentley-badged state limousine ever delivered to British royalty.

Chief Executive Graham Morris had been an early victim of the corporate upheavals of 1998. He had every cause to be unhappy about this, because he had masterminded the introduction of the new Arnage/Silver

Pit stop action, during the night, at Le Mans in 2001, when one of the Bentley Speed 8s called in for a fuel and driver change.

In 2003, Bentley took first and second places in the Le Mans 24 Hour race, the winning car being crewed by Rinaldo Capello, Tom Kristensen and Guy Smith. Later the winning car drove down Paris' Champs Elysees, with vintage Bentleys behind it.

Once VW took control of Bentley, it decided to set up a race program to gain valuable publicity. The EXP Speed 8 cars were based on existing Audi racecar technology (Audi was also a VW subsidiary), and were mainly intended for the Le Mans 24 Hour Race. The Speed 8s took third place in 2001, fourth in 2002, but took fantastic first and second places in 2003 – after which the program was wound up.

Seraph models, along with the complete modernization of the Crewe plant. Even so, he was not officially replaced until early in 1999, when Tony Gott (the technical supremo behind the Bentley Arnage project)

took over that post.

VW was not long in formulating its new strategy for the future of Bentley. Although they would naturally carry on building the Arnage, and indeed would push

on with the development of faster and more advanced types, they had already decided to produce a brand new type of Bentley which would have no technical links with the past.

VWs far-reaching program, it said, would cost approximately $800 million of investment capital. Within three years, VW emphasized, they would invest more in Bentley than the Vickers organization had invested in the whole of its 18-year tenure. The centerpiece of this massive investment would be the progressive introduction of new models, which would rely on VW-Audi engineering. These new cars, they made clear, would be more technically advanced that ever, and would be the fastest Bentleys ever put on sale.

This brave and aggressive stance was meant to shock the die-hards who had already suggested that VW, whose "people cars" included 21 million rear-engined, air-cooled Beetles, was about to degrade a legendary brand. VW had every right, they thought, to point out: "Look, we spent $688 million to buy the company, and we are committed to spending another half-billion to revitalize it. We're serious about Bentley's future."

VW might also have pointed out that they had already moved to rescue, revive and to reinvent the Italian Bugatti and Lamborghini concerns – both of them in the "Supercar" business, and both of them in deep financial trouble. In both cases, these companies were thriving under VW-Audi ownership.

Apart from its decision to design, develop, and build

This study of the Continental GT makes it look small – but in fact it was 15 feet, 9 inches long – and had a top speed of over 190 miles per hour.

Below: Do you remember the days when cars had separate and obvious bumpers? No sign of them, of course, on the Bentley Continental GT, which also featured carefully recessed tail lamps.

Left: Bentley designers had a difficult job in shaping the new Continental GT, for tradition had to be blended with modern aerodynamic efficiency.

Two aspects of the fascia/instrument panel and driving compartment of the Bentley Continental GT, which went on sale at the end of 2002.

a totally new Bentley, VW wanted to sell many more of them. By projecting a much cheaper selling price for the new car, it was making a well-financed "dash for growth," and was not about to meekly follow in the old tradition. Crewe, it suggested, would be much-modernized complex (even though the new Arnage/Silver Seraph facilities were ultramodern), which could produce up to 10,000 Bentleys a year. This would make all previous Bentley achievements look like peanuts.

Not even the mighty VW, though, could impose such a revolutionary strategy at once, and it was always clear that it would develop in several phases. The first, which had been thrust upon the new owners by the bad-tempered corporate battle with BMW (in fairness, most independent financial experts think that this was badly handled by Vickers, who never made the trademark ownership situation clear in the first place), was to begin to slowly distance the Crewe complex from BMW influence and involvement.

In fact, BMW was much more closely involved with the Arnage/Silver Seraph models than it first appeared, for there were many hidden BMW components. The front seats, for instance, were based on a BMW design.) In simple terms, though, VW had to bite the bullet, accept BMW as a medium-term supplier of parts; to reinstate (and substitute) up-dated "classic" V-8 engines in place of BMW power units; and to begin sidelining the Rolls-Royce brand at the expense of Bentley.

VW next had to reemphasize and enhance the Bentley brand in the market place – and one decision was to do this by bringing the "Bentley" name back into long-distance sports car racing, thus reviving "Golden Age" memories of Bentley's great achievements at Le Mans, Brooklands, and other locations, in the "vintage" era. There was never any intention of trying to build racing cars at Crewe. The expertise was simply not available. VW intended to import Audi expertise from Germany and build cars based on Audi layouts. Race preparation and management would be by the best and most experienced independent personalities available. The last, the most ambitious, the most costly – and the most critical part of the program – would be to initiate the all-new model lineup, which had been rumored since the takeover battle began. Not only was VW determined to use the high-powered engines, and the very advanced technology that was already available in Germany, but it was also intent on boosting sales by driving down the selling price of new models.

To do this, VW approved the start of an aggressive design and engineering program, though at the same time the still-novel Arnage model would remain on sale. First, VW reacted to customer comments by somehow managing to insert the old V-8 engine (this became the Arnage Red Label) into the existing body shell, and there would be other evolutions to follow that – notably the Arnage L and Arnage T.

Even so, the real future, as they saw it, was to commission an all-new project, one that was initially known only as the MSB (Medium Sized Bentley). To do this, and to make sure that it really was a fresh start, VW needed new design and style thinking. Dirk van Braeckel was drafted in from Germany (where he had already rejuvenated the image of the Skoda), along with Dr. Ulrich Hackenberg, who became its technical director. Van Braeckel arrived in March 1999, moved very fast, and by the end of the year the lines, and the general format of the MSB project, had all been agreed.

For the next two years, the motoring press went off into a feeding frenzy, picking up and running with whatever rumors that it could find. Even so, it was 2002 before Bentley officially hinted at what they had been working on for some time, and even then very few technical details were released.

A new "cheaper" Bentley, the "Continental GT," was unveiled in the autumn of 2002, series production would begin in 2003, and volume sales ("volume," that is, by previous Bentley standards) would start before the end of that year.

In spite of the urgency to transform Bentley's prospects, it had taken a full five years (1998 to 2003) to move from the original merger, to the launch of a new model. In the meantime, VW continued to pump financial investment into Crewe, this largesse becoming more and clear as the days rolled on. More than $21 million was spent on a new chrome and wood workshop. Expansion of the existing design center went ahead. VW also committed $90 million to a revitalization of the Crewe plant, which had already had much money spent on it to launch the Arnage/ Rolls-Royce Silver Seraph.

At the same time the rumors about future products – all to be VW based – began to spread. The first new car, it was said, would "only" cost about $120,000 (which was Porsche pricing for a full four-seater coupe – but it proved to be a substantial underestimate), and before long it would be joined by a more conventional four-door sedan. And after that?

If component sharing was not thought to be a problem, the entire worldwide VW/Audi "parts bin" could be plundered.

Bentley designers considered everything, the layout and labeling of the twin-turbo V-8 engine of the Arnage T, and the switch gear of the late 1990s cars.

Bentley's new management made no attempt to defend themselves against the die-hards who suggested that this might kill the brand. But after all, those with exceptional memories (or a good library) could hark back to the early 1930s, when the arrival of the first "Rolls-Bentley" was thought to be a complete and disastrous change from the W.O. Bentleys of the 1920s.

The newly focused Bentley management was sure its approach was correct. From a very early stage, rumors began to spread – that an all-new Bentley would be given four-wheel drive, not merely to harness the immense power which was sure to be available, but because VW-Audi already had well-proven, robust, and astonishingly effective four-wheel drive systems that

could do a wonderful job on future models.

In the meantime, the time came for VW Chairman, Ferdinand Piech to retire, and well before that time he made it clear that he wanted Bernd Pichetsrieder to be his successor. This, incidentally, was the same man who had been working at BMW in 1998, and had robbed him of the Rolls-Royce brand.

After VW had bought the company, and to keep the publicity pot boiling, they commissioned this one-off concept car which was labeled Bentley Hunaudieres. Under the skin, it was based on the chassis of the four-wheel drive Lamborghini Diablo (this was another marque owned by VW-Audi), but the car was powered by a unique VW W-16 engine.

The wide and flat rear view of the Hunaudieres concept coupe hides the engine, which was a 64-valve W-16 engine by VW. Except for the EXP Speed 8 race cars, this was certainly the fastest Bentley built – so far.

Left: This idiosyncratic fascia style was used in the one-off Bentley Hunaudieres concept coupe.

Below: The engine of the Hunaudieres concept coupe was a one-off 64-valve W-16 monster, which produced (a claimed) 623 horsepower. In effect, this was really two ultranarrow angle V-8 engines mounted at 72 degrees on a common crankcase. Many technical and component features would be shared with the engines to be fitted to the forthcoming Continental GT road car.

This duly came about. Pischetsrieder took over as chairman of the VW Group, and it was under his overall control the very last Crewe-built Rolls-Royce was completed on August 30, 2002 – after which the company operating the site became Bentley Motors Ltd.

In the meantime, VW had shown off the Bentley Hunaudieres project car, which excited every red-blooded car enthusiast, though it was never intended to be other than a flag-waving exercise.

The Hunaudieres (the name was lifted from a section of the Le Mans motor racing circuit) was a statement of technical ability, not of intent – that Bentley staff could now develop any type of new model. Launched in 1999, this was a one-off coupe, a big, impressive, and smoothly shaped midengined two-seater that was fitted with a specially designed VW 620 horsepower 8.0-liter W-16 power unit. To save time, Bentley based it on the four-wheel drive chassis and structure of the Lamborghini Diablo VT. (As we know, Lamborghini was also part of the VW Group.)

The engine, a 72-degree 8-liter "W-16," was a distant relative of the 2.8/3.2-litre VR6 engine of the VW Golf. Eventually, it also became "Big Brother" to the W-12s that would go into other new models, including the forthcoming Bentley Continental GT road car.

The Continental Flying Spur saloon, new in 2005, was a bulky but pleasingly detailed four-door saloon, with colossal performance. By any standards, this was to be the flagship of the contemporary Bentley range.

Although it caused a stir, Bentley never suggested that the car would ever go on sale, and little test running of the prototype was ever carried out. Certainly, the Continental GT, which would appear in 2002, was an entirely different machine.

By this time, VW had made it clear that they wanted to expand Bentley, and to bring down prices. To do this, an entirely different type of Bentley-badged model would need to be developed. Even so, VW could not justify the engineering of an all-new car.

There would not even be a new engine and chassis. Instead, a lot of "parts bin" engineering would take place, the inference being that a new Bentley would have to use an already-projected VW or Audi platform. Not only were there several of these, but an astonishing new range of petrol and diesel engines – using three, four, five, six, eight, ten, twelve and even sixteen cylinder formations.

Once Dr. Hackenberg took over at Crewe, industry watchers saw what might follow, for one of his previous assignments had been to evolve the super-luxury VW "Concept D" car. Much larger than any previous VW, it

From the nose to the screen (including everything hidden away under the hood) the 2005 Flying Spur shared its engineering and lines with the Continental GT Coupe, but behind that was a full four-seater/four-door sedan car.

This was the front seat and driving compartment of the 2005-model Bentley Continental Flying Spur.

used a front-mounted engine and four-wheel drive. One "Concept D" was a unique W-12 (effectively two of the ultranarrow angle, 15-degree, VR6 engines, mounted in 72-degree vee, on a new crankcase).

The original D1 W-12 engine was rated at 415 horsepower/5.6-liters, but within a year it had improved to 450 horsepower/6.0-liters. When D1 finally became the Phaeton in 2002, and built in a new factory in Dresden, it had been derated to 414 horsepower/5,998 cc.

The new-generation Bentley, to be previewed in 2002, would use a shortened version of the platform of the Phaeton. The W-12 engine would be turbocharged, and it would be monstrously powerful. Bentley body shells would use floorpan assemblies and internal panels provided from Dresden, would use the Phaeton's four-wheel drive system and similar suspension, though with air springing. The projected top speed, close to 200 miles per hour, made this the fastest Bentley road car of all time.

The wraps came off in October 2002, when the new

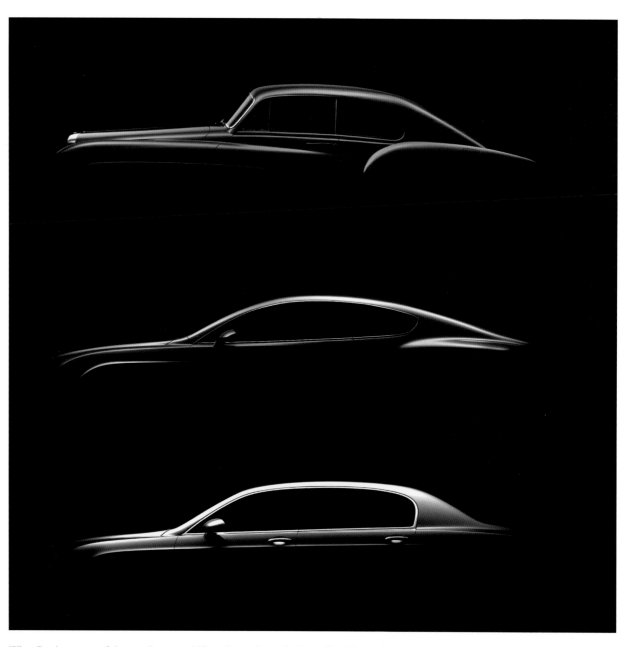

When Bentley previewed the new Continental Flying Spur sedan in 2005, it offered this triple silhouette, which showed how the shape of the original Continental R of 1952 (top) had influenced that of the Coupe of 2002 (center) and the Flying Spur (2005). The styling "cues" are clear.

This tail view (above) and pure side view of the Bentley Continental GT completely hide the VW ancestry of the running gear. There is absolutely no evidence of the use of four-wheel drive.

In 2002, every detail of the new-generation Bentley Continental was lovingly crafted, including the fascia/instrument panel layout, the door "furniture," and the wheels themselves.

Bentley "Continental GT" went on show at the Paris salon, as a massive, but graceful, two-plus-two coupe, with the W-12 engine, four-wheel drive, and a ZF six-speed automatic transmission. The style was at once rather brutal, but totally new and uncompromising. Somehow the designers had managed to preserve a nose that looked as a modern Bentley should look, though with a streamlined shape. This mostly steel monocoque had an aluminum hood pressing, and composite front fenders. Naturally there were no bumpers, while two big oval exhaust outlets told their own story.

Inside the cabin, and absolutely as expected from a

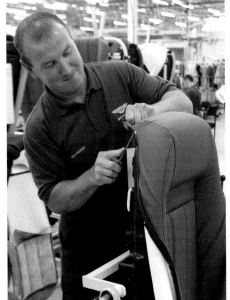

car that was born at Crewe, there was wall-to-wall walnut, high-quality carpet, and high-grade leather. Satellite navigation was standard. Little of the engine was exposed when the hood was lifted, but twin turbochargers and intercoolers helped boost peak power to 552 horsepower at 6,100 rpm. All-independent suspension was as effective as expected – and it was altogether typical of the development team

that there were four driver-adjustable ride settings – Comfort, Normal, Sport One and Sport Two.

All this, and a 196-mile per hour top speed, was available in Britain for a mere $176,000 or so – which compared with $373,000 for a Bentley Continental T, or $253,000 asked for an Aston Martin Vanquish. So, could Bentley sell the 3,500 or more new Continental GTs every year as they were forecasting? Adrian Hallmark, sales and marketing director, certainly thought so:

"Price isn't the main consideration in this market. When there are only three or four players in a luxury sector, it's more the brand that makes the difference."

When production cars finally began to leave Crewe in mid-2003, Bentley claimed an order bank of 4,000, with some markets quoting 2005 as the earliest time that any new client could expect to take delivery. A few doubters originally suggested that the new Bentley was misconceived. They were soon proved wrong.

Since the entire commercial future of Bentley rested on this chassis, the arrival of a sedan version was inevitable, this duly appearing in January 2005. To be called the Continental Flying Spur, this was a four-door five-seater derivative of the Continental GT, a technical and marketing move, which bore a striking resemblance to something a previous Bentley management had done – in 1957, when the Flying Spur had grown out of the Continental S-Type.

Although it was considerably longer than the GT (the wheelbase had gone up by no less than 12.6 inches – it was now longer even than the lengthened-wheelbase VW Phaeton), and was therefore a lot heavier at 5,500 pounds, the new-type Flying Spur was still sure to be a very fast car, for with the same engine tune as the GT (now quoted at 560 horsepower) it could reach nearly 190 miles per hour.

In style, the front end of the new sedan looked almost exactly like the GT. Bentley claimed there were differences almost everywhere, for this was a full five-seater sedan, with a massive trunk. In fact, no less than 60 per cent of the new car – mechanical, bodywork, and details – was shared with that of the GT.

For the moment – and only for the moment, for a convertible version of the GT was also forecast to be under way – this was the flagship of the "VW-Bentley" range, and was set to sell at $184,000 when deliveries began in mid-2005. If demand was high enough, the rumors went, assembly of the Flying Spur – or part-assembly, at least – might even take place alongside the VW Phaeton, in Dresden.

Old and new: a 1929 Rolls-Royce frames a new Bentley GT.

The Bentley story, therefore, was neither at its end, nor even at a new beginning, for at this time the new management was still forging ahead with a massive re-alignment program for this prestige marque. Would VW eventually reach their target, of selling 10,000 Bentleys every year? By 2005/2006 it looked as if they might.

CHAPTER *Eight*

ROLLS-ROYCE FOR THE 2000S

BMW'S NEW STRATEGY

FOR BMW, IT TOOK NEARLY FIVE AGONIZINGLY LONG YEARS BEFORE IT COULD REALLY GET ITS HANDS ON ROLLS-ROYCE. Although it took control of the Rolls-Royce brand in mid-1998, this was a delayed deal. While VW would keep on building "old-style" (Silver Seraph) Rolls-Royce cars until mid-2002, BMW could not start to do so until January 1, 2003. Not only that, but contractually they were also obliged to say nothing (officially, that is) about their intentions for a new model until then.

Behind the scenes, of course, a great deal could be done. Not only could design and engineering work on a new car begin at once, but because the brand would have to leave Crewe, a search could start for a factory in which to build the new model. But would all this be done in Germany or Great Britain?

To their credit, BMW soon decided that the car should be shaped in England, and that the cars should be built in the marque's home country. Design work, therefore, started in hired premises in London, and after a long delay, BMW also chose a factory site at Goodwood, Sussex, south of London.

When it opened up in 2002, the brand-new Goodwood factory was only Rolls-Royce's fourth home in a century of car production.

Factories somehow don't look like factories these days – this was Goodwood in the early 2000s.

Above: BMW acquired the rights to manufacture Rolls-Royce cars beginning January 1, 2003, and was immediately able to announce a brand new car, which was powered by a 6.75-liter BMW V-12 engine which produced 460 horsepower. The front-end style was unashamedly "retro," with rectangular headlamps that did not altogether match up the rest of the lines.

Left: The first BMW-owned Rolls-Royce was the Phantom of 2003, with a 460 horsepower V-12 engine, a top speed of 150 miles per hour, all in a 5,500 pound automobile with a 140-inch wheelbase and a massively comfortable cabin. Production built up slowly, but no fewer than 700 Phantoms were produced in 2004.

It was the factory location, more than the engineering of the new model, that caused the most controversy. Encouraged by that arch motor sport enthusiast Lord March (whose two events, the Goodwood Festival of Speed, and the Goodwood Revival Meeting, were centerpieces of his Goodwood estate's activities), BMW pinpointed a site less than two miles from the historic motor racing circuit on his

No matter what the background, noone could mistake the nose of the new Rolls-Royce Phantom.

estate. The site had once been used for extracting material from the ground, and was currently derelict. BMW proposed to erect a factory that was to be constructed partially underground, a building that was to be so carefully landscaped that it would be virtually invisible from the surrounding area.

Even so, although this was perfect for providing new employment, and for bringing great prestige to this part of England, environmentalists and other anti-industry die-hards fought tooth-and-nail to have the factory proposal killed off. It was only after much delay – and BMW's threat to take the entire project back to Germany – that the local authority gave approval. Construction began in mid-2001, and the $104 million building was completed before the end of 2002 – just in

Although the Phantom was very large and bulky, it was fast, and handled remarkably well.

time for BMW to hire 350 staff, take charge of the brand, and to show off the new model.

True to its obligations, BMW had nothing to say about a new car until January 2003, but there were ample controlled "leaks" – just enough to give the pundits something to consider. Right from the start, it was clear that the new-generation Rolls-Royce would be even larger, more powerful, faster and – by definition – more expensive than the last of the Crewe-built Silver Seraphs. Not only that, but it soon became apparent that almost all of the running gear – engine, transmission, suspension, and other chassis equipment – would be lifted directly from BMW's existing top-of-the-line models. One quirky little detail was that the wheel centers were crowned by the familiar "RR" trademark symbols. But these plates were floated, and weighted, so that they always ran in the correct, vertical mode. Neat. And typical of BMW's attention to detail on this car.

One thing was certain. Except for the use of the brand name, along with the famous Spirit of Ecstasy emblem, and the equally legendary "RR" badges, there would be virtually no marketing connection with any previous Rolls-Royce. Though BMW would carry on using its own engines, the Silver Seraph platform and suspension was not available, and they certainly had no desire to use that style in any case.

After a great deal of thought, BMW's strategic decision was to base the running gear of the new Rolls-Royce on that of the BMW 760, which was due to meet its public in late 2002 – V-12 engine, six-speed automatic transmission, and all – while the next was to establish the style, bulk, and character of the new BMW-RR machine.

There was an underlying agreement that any new Rolls-Royce should include a great deal of "Britishness" – not only in what it looked like, but what its interior and equipment contained. Accordingly, the company searched the London metropolitan area, and finally settled on renting part of a one-time bank building north of London's Hyde Park. By the beginning of

1999, BMW's design director, Chris Bangle, (himself British) installed Ian Cameron and a 20-strong multinational design team to evolve the shape.

Their immediate "given" was the need to build a car on a 140.5-inch wheelbase, and to allow for optional 21-inch road wheels, so the new car – soon called "Phantom" (no other numbers were necessary) – was bound to be colossal. By the end of 1999, the shape of a massive four-door machine had been chosen, one whose radiator shell was four inches taller than that of the Silver Seraph, whose nose was uncompromisingly vertical, and which promised to weighed no less than 5,500 pounds. Even though the nose featured rectangular headlamps, and threatened to have all the aerodynamic qualities of a barn door, BMW claimed a drag coefficient of only 0.383.

This, and several other mind-blowing production statistics made one realize how ambitious BMW/Rolls-Royce really was. At 19 feet 1.6 inches long, the car outstretched the Silver Seraph by 18 inches, it had the tallest tires used on any production car, and the initial price of $384,000 (before adding any of the many seductive extras) was much higher than the final Silver Seraph price of $270,000.

The only modern car likely to match up was the new

Mercedes-Benz-inspired Maybach – and somehow this car could not match the timeless quality of the new product from Goodwood. BMW knew that the Maybach had been developed, almost in a fit of pique from Daimler-Benz, when they had lost the Rolls-Royce/Bentley engine deal in 1994.

Interior equipment, predictably, was as sumptuous as ever – a fascinating amalgam of traditional Rolls-Royce values, with a great deal of BMW 7-Series equipment included, or hidden away, but still doing an appropriate job.

As one road tester commented when he drove the car:

"The 7-Series influences are clear and aren't confined to the [ignition] key; the start-up procedure, the operation of the gear and indicator stalks, the simplified iDrive and even the bongs and chimes are familiar. But it's all in the background: nothing you can see or touch is remotely 7-influenced . . ."

One fascinating detail was that the new Phantom had rear-hinged ("suicide") rear doors, though BMW was quick to point out that when the car was moving these were automatically locked, and could not be over-ridden by the passengers.

Technically, of course, the new Phantom leaned heavily on the latest BMW technology, by using a

Massive and rather angular, the longer-wheelbase Phantom of 2005 was sure to sell steadily.

sophisticated aluminum unit-construction body/chassis space frame, of a type that had first been seen on the limited-production BMW Z8 roadster. Many of the skin panels, too, were in aluminum, though the front fenders were in sheet-molded composite material.

Mechanically, there was much 7-Series hidden away, including the twin-overhead-camshaft-per-bank 453 horsepower/6749 cc V-12 engine, a six-speed ZF automatic transmission, and independent suspension front and rear, with air springs and self-leveling, all

allied to light, power-assisted steering. The disc brakes, incidentally, were no less than 14.6 inches in diameter.

Seeing the cars being assembled at Goodwood emphasized how this was no longer a British, but an Anglo-German, project. The manufacturing process started with complete but bare aluminum bodies being transported, three at a time, by truck, from BMW's Dingolfing factory (northeast of Munich, in Germany). Engines and transmissions also came from Bavaria, the balance of the 2,500 parts flowing in from all over Europe, the UK, and even the United States.

At Goodwood, though, the bodies were painted, assembled, and completely furnished, with the highest-quality wood, leather, and carpets that one would expect of a car like this. This was a new model, of course, on which a great deal was riding. BMW, after all, had dabbled (admittedly, at a different level) with realigning Rover in its own image, and failed. At this very top level, it simply could not be seen to fall down at all.

Seeing the new Phantom as a direct competitor only to the new Maybach (on which much, too, was riding in Stuttgart), the media looked very carefully at the new Phantom before passing judgment. Happily, they seemed to be content with the build quality, the specification, and the behavior of the Phantom, though the front-end style was definitely found to be an acquired taste.

It was, of course, a very fast and expensive-to-run car. It had a top speed of almost 150 miles per hour (it would surely have been a lot higher but for that bluff nose, and the use of electronic limiting of the power output). It could be cruised at 120 miles per hour and more in almost complete silence . . . where traffic laws were favorable. Best, though, to ignore the fuel consumption, which was no better than 12 miles per gallon.

Britain's *Autocar* magazine got it right, surely, by summarizing its test with: "It's an imposing, beautifully made – if not beautiful – object, a real Rolls-Royce, and right first time."

Not that it was ever likely to sell in large numbers. In 2003, when production was still ramping up, only 502 cars rolled out of the door at Goodwood, but 700 followed in 2004, and an annual target of at least 1,000 began to look feasible in later years.

In the meantime, rumors of additional models turned into sightings, and sightings turned into official statements, for BMW clearly intended to expand the Phantom range in exactly the same way as the previous management always had.

Even so, at the Geneva Motor Show in March 2004, the introduction of 100EX, a massive cabriolet concept car, caused a real stir. Hard-bitten motoring writers were startled, not by the style, and not by the sheer size of the machine – but by the fact that it was powered by a 9.0-liter V-16 engine.

Because the structure and style of the new car was almost as expected, the engine made most headlines. Yet some writers who had visited the BMW museum in Munich, had seen an earlier-generation engine like this, which had once been squeezed into a 7-Series sedan for testing. In that 7-Series, the engine seemed to be so large that the water-cooling radiators had needed to be relocated in the trunk, but in 100EX the whole car was designed around it. The engine was one of several ongoing projects that BMW had in process, and it was closely related to the V-12 (which was fitted to normal Phantoms).

Although 100EX was a concept, no more and no less, it signaled BMW's advanced thinking, for there was a new type of aluminum space-frame structure, a style which (though created by BMW's Designworks in California) definitely nodded to the latest Crewe-type Corniche of 2000-2002, and the use of rear-hinged doors, which were intended to ease access to the rear seats. There was a new front-end treatment, which seemed to be more pleasing than the "cliff-face" style of the Phantom, and the inclusion of a teak surround over the rear tonneau, luxury yacht style, was a nice touch.

According to Rolls-Royce in March 2004, 100EX

was only an experimental project, completed to celebrate the centenary of Rolls-Royce cars, but by the end of the year the company had given approval to a production version of this machine. Not expected to be available until 2007, this was to be a smaller car than 100EX, and would use the Phantom's 6.75-liter V-12 engine. It was expected to cost at least $480,000, might be named "Corniche" (surprise, surprise . . .), and would be built in very limited quantities.

The arrival of a longer-wheelbase version of the Phantom was more widely expected, for such a machine was somewhat easier to engineer. Previewed in March 2005, but with deliveries due to begin later in the year, the stretched Phantom limousine looked almost exactly like the "normal" Phantom, except that it had a 10-inch longer wheelbase.

All that extra length was concentrated in the rear floor/door/roof area, so that rear seat legroom was much increased, this meaning that changes to the aluminum space frame were also needed in that area. For those who needed to count the cost, those extra ten inches were thought likely to add $64,000 – or, to put it crudely, $6,400 per inch.

For the time being, it seemed, BMW had been content to allow ex-Rolls-Royce-Crewe personality Tony Gott to run the show at Goodwood, just as he had in the prelaunch and buildup stage, but from mid-2004 Gott was abruptly replaced by Karl-Heinz Kalbfell, a long-time top man from BMW itself (and even he walked away before the end of the year). Gott, it seems, had not been easy in his relations with other German personalities, so he had to go. From that moment, therefore, Rolls-Royce became an integral part of the BMW empire, with cars engineered by Germans, and with the business run by Germans. Only the assembly process itself was now British.

This story, however, was always evolving. Rolls-Royce watchers knew, full well, that BMW was determined to tap in to every possible corner of the luxury car market. So extra derivatives on the Phantom theme were to be expected as the 2000s progressed.

More than 100 years after the Rolls-Royce marque had been created, the brand, its standing, and its image, were totally different. In that time there had been three owners. The cars had been produced on five sites, and the Bentley brand had come and gone. What on earth might happen in the next 10 years, or even in the next generation?

INDEX

Aknowledgements

The Publishers and the Author would like to thank the following for their help in preparing this book.

Graham Roper for allowing us to photograph his Bentley GT

Sargeants of Goudhurst for allowing us to photograph the 1929 Rolls-Royce 20 Horsepower and the $3^1/2$ liter Bentley

Rolls-Royce Motor Cars, Press Club

Audi-VW Corporate Archive

James Mann Photography

Nick Whitman for the 1929 Rolls-Royce Springfield